Please Return to
BRIAN
MAHOOD

The Number One Success System
to Boost Your Earnings
in Real Estate

The Number One Success System

to Boost Your Earnings

in Real Estate

EDWARD F. RYBKA

PRENTICE-HALL, INC.   Englewood Cliffs, N.J

PRENTICE-HALL INTERNATIONAL, INC., *London*
PRENTICE-HALL OF AUSTRALIA, PTY. LTD., *Sydney*
PRENTICE-HALL OF CANADA, LTD., *Toronto*
PRENTICE-HALL OF INDIA PRIVATE LTD., *New Delhi*
PRENTICE-HALL OF JAPAN, INC., *Tokyo*

Library of Congress
Catalog Card Number: 78-147866

Twelfth Printing . . . . . August, 1979

PRINTED IN THE UNITED STATES OF AMERICA
ISBN-0-13-626473-5
B & P

Dedication

To my darling wife, Irene, and our
children, Edward William, Robert Stephen
and Michelle Renee, without whose help
and encouragement this book would surely
not have been written.

A Word from the Author . . .

When I was 22 and anxious to get ahead, I was doing accounting for a Cleveland-based steel company. One night, after a particularly tedious day, I read about the sale of the Empire State Building in my evening newspaper. What especially caught my attention was the fact that the sale of the world's tallest building resulted in a sales commission of one million dollars.

Imagine that! A cool million for just one transaction!

I decided that if that kind of money could be made in real estate, I was wasting my time keeping books. Besides, I knew in my heart it would be more fun and more challenging to deal with people than with ledgers.

I quickly obtained a real estate license and spent the next three years learning the practical side of selling property. In the first six months, I earned $8,000. My commission reached $12,000 in my second year and in my third and last year as a salesman, my earnings were over $16,000.

Then, in 1956, I opened my first small office. Six years later, the first of six branch offices was opened.

Two subjects from my college days helped tremendously: Marketing and Psychology. Using the basic principles from these courses, my company grew and outstanding sales records were compiled. I discovered that education and low turnover in personnel are the principal reasons for a continuing increase in sales and lasting success in real estate endeavors.

By 1964, our 28-man staff (15 of whom were brokers) organized its own sales clinic to develop a sales procedure that would guarantee success. Success, that is, for all who would follow our blueprint.

For seven weeks—three hours a day each week—salesmen were assigned to report on various books. These were books designed to improve work habits and control of time as well as sales and closing techniques. Such extensive self-education was hard work, but all of our men participated in it enthusiastically.

Next, we put these eagerly sought principles to work. The result? Our company sold more than 800 homes in one year for an exciting total of $18,000,000. That was an increase of 40% over the company's previous annual volume. Furthermore, earnings of the staff jumped from $12,000 a year to an average of more than $16,000, and our new men immediately started earning the high averages.

I attribute the success of my firm to the staff's INSIDE SECRETS—in the BASIC FUNDAMENTALS and PRE-VIOUSLY UNKNOWN TECHNIQUES of successful real estate sales procedure. These methods are all in this book. Now, for the first time, we are sharing the Rybka method with interested people like you.

Let me emphasize that predictable sales success in real estate awaits ALL who have the know-how and will to get ahead. The goal of this book, therefore, is to give you all of the tools that you will need to achieve such success.

For example, consider only a few of the features you will find clearly explained in this book:

• It will show you how to master your time with a foolproof schedule which allows you to be in the right place at the right time.

• It will provide you with twenty-two approaches for getting the seller to list his property with you.

• It will provide you with a proven formula for breaking sales slumps—a problem all salesmen seem to encounter at one time or another.

• It will provide you with a simple method for adjusting the overpriced listing—a technique that is virtually guaranteed to increase sales.

• It will show you how to use the eight big emotional appeals that every prospective buyer responds to and, most important, *cannot* control.

• It will show you how to use "sales conditioners" with all qualified prospects to ensure speedy, favorable decisions.

• It will show you how to apply *terrific* pressure in closing a sale; the type of pressure that steadily, determinedly demands positive action.

My system is based on proven fundamentals which constitute the knowledge needed to sell real estate successfully. By following this system faithfully, you will be well on your way to multiplying your earnings.

Edward F. Rybka

ACKNOWLEDGMENTS

Grateful acknowledgment is made to the 33 members of the 1963 Rybka Realty team for their many kindnesses in sharing many of the original success-tested sales techniques that not one man in a hundred had ever heard of.

Acknowledgment also is made to Bob Brennan, Real Estate Editor of *The Cleveland Press*, for planting the idea for this book.

Contents

*You CAN Earn $16,000 or More—Every Year
• Phenomenal Growth of Rybka Realty Inc.
• The Key to Success—Training in Fundamentals*

*Systematize Daily Activities • Develop a Clientele
• Sell Yourself • Slumps • Send Brochures
• Become Known! • Speak Correctly
• Want to Be a Failure?*

The Foundation for the Real Estate Industry Is the

Size Decision • Checking on Personnel • Turn-over Is to Be Expected • Promote from Within • What Women Mean to the Company • Training on the Job • Importance of the Manager

List of Exhibits

17

*The Number One Success System
to Boost Your Earnings
in Real Estate*

Chapter One

You CAN Earn More

Everybody in the real estate business knows that there is a shortage of salesmen; of trained, dedicated, enthusiastic, self-propelled producers. And in the next decade the World War II baby boom will emerge as an army of eager house hunters. The demand for highly-qualified sales personnel will reach its highest level in matching the greatest real estate boom in our country's history.

Virtually everyone in the real estate field works on commission and the most common rate of commission currently is 7% of a property's sales price. Most full-time salesmen earn $5000 to $10,000 a year. Beginners usually make less, but many well-trained, experienced salesmen earn $16,000 or more annually.

That $16,000 figure is the goal of this book. I am going to show you; indeed, I am going to prove to you that you, too, can earn $16,000 or more each and every year that you are in the real estate business.

To illustrate, Exhibit 1-1 shows the exact formula to be used in making $16,000 a year.

I know that you can earn this amount because each of my salesmen has proven that my system works You will find a complete job description of the Rybka salesman in a later chapter, but let me point out briefly that the Rybka Man is

---

Exhibit 1-1

FORMULA FOR MAKING
$16,000 A YEAR

You must make 30 sales with an average
commission of $300 per sale.   30 x $300 = $ 9,000.

You must have 40 listings sell with an
average listing fee of $175   40 x $175 = $ 7,000.
                                                          $16,000.

Steps to Attain This Goal

1. If you sell two prospects out of 30 calls or leads you receive, then
to make 30 sales, you must call two prospects each working day, or
600 prospects a year.
2. To have 40 listings sell, you must list 66 houses. If it takes 30
seller contacts to get two listings, then you must see 900 sellers a
year, or an average of three sellers each working day.

Daily Work Plan to Make $16,000

1. You must call or search for two buyers each working day!
2. You must talk to three sellers each working day!

A SIMPLE FORMULA IN WHICH EVERY HOUR INVESTED
MEANS YOU WIN!!

---

respected as an individual, yet he is expected to be a member of
the team and he must adhere to the rules we have devised to
ensure his personal success and the success of our company.

We don't coddle a man, nor do we tolerate mediocrity. We
insist that each of our men make at least one sale per month,
without exception.

The Rybka Man is successful because he is required to·

1. Be a creative thinker.
2. Get all the facts about each property.
3. Get an exclusive listing of the property.
·4. Prepare facts in sales presentation form.
5. See prospective purchasers and make presentations accord-
    ing to an experience-dictated schedule.

6. Continue to make presentations until he sells the property.[1]

Our philosophy is that we can only build a stronger company by attracting and holding men of the highest caliber. We feel that we can accomplish this through:

1. Proper planning.
2. Adequate advice.
3. Dedication and demonstration.
4. Inspired leadership.[2]

We also ask for some special functions from the Rybka Man. Among these, he is required to:

1. Inspect all new listings in his service area within 48 hours and submit his personal appraisal to the man who listed the property.
2. Tour his assigned area each Monday.
3. Call each seller every Wednesday.
4. Call buyers weekly.
5. Balance his floor time with an equal amount of missionary work outside.
6. Scan all realty ads daily.
7. Address and mail sales literature weekly.
8. Complete an advertising-results form daily.
9. Help his fellow salesmen in listing or selling, when needed.
10. Report promptly when scheduled for floor duty.

Are you wondering, still, if my system really works?

I organized Rybka Realty Inc. in 1956. Since then, it has been expanded into seven offices with 43 salesmen. It has set an enviable record of more than 7600 used home sales, totaling $143,400,000. Recently, in a depressed real estate market in greater Cleveland, the Rybka Company made history by exceeding its past records. It scored 1055 sales for $21,606,000, making it the leader in home sales in the Cleveland area. Truly, it is one of the nation's outstanding residential real estate firms.

---

[1]Excerpt from the pamphlet: *Objectives, Means and How of Selling Real Estate,* by Bob Bale; published by Bob Bale Institute, 4710 N. 16th St., Phoenix, Arizona.

[2]Bob Bale, *Objectives, Means and How of Selling Real Estate.*

Furthermore, the theories and procedures which spell success for the Rybka Company were developed by two basic methods:

Exhibit 1-2 shows how Rybka Realty's sales record was used by *The Cleveland Press* for a sales promotion flyer.[3] *The Press's* sales department suggested to builders and other brokers that they emulate Rybka Realty Co.

1. **Outside Help**—Many hours were spent absorbing both a general and a real estate education in colleges; on sales training and personality development programs such as those offered by Dale Carnegie; at many seminars and with many publications, including that great book, *Brass Tacks of Selling* by Ray Smith, plus the anticipated period of trial and error.

2. **Inside Help**—Our own Rybka Realty sales-boosting educational seminar was organized in 1963. Briefly, each of our then 33 full-time salesmen, who for years had consistently earned more than the high average of the industry, was asked to participate in this seven-day, theory-and-practice brain session. These men related their actual sales experiences, referred to general sales theories and revised them to create the Rybka Method of Successful Selling which is condensed in this present book.

When the Rybka Method is studied and its principles are followed, both the newcomers and the veterans in real estate sales will be on their way to earning $16,000 or more a year.

Fundamentals and knowledge are needed to sell real estate. Your objective, of course, is to earn money because:

a. You want to supply your family with a good living,

b. You wish to have security and happiness, or

c. You want to provide the necessities of life.

Please remember that in spite of the fact that you are or will be working for an organization, you are your own Board of Directors. You are your own boss, ready and capable to determine your own policies and to direct your own energies.

---

[3]Reprinted with the permission of *The Cleveland Press,* 901 Lakeside Ave., Cleveland, Ohio.

25

Again, you are your own staff with awesome self responsibility to determine what type of job you are doing; to determine, in the final analysis, whether or not you will be a success or a failure.

All I can do is to aid and advise, suggest, help, assist, counsel and hope you do the things which are necessary to be a successful real estate man.

However, if you still have doubts—if you are pondering the road to failure—you are on your own. The man who would fail must fail alone because nobody will teach him how to do it.

Your objective is and must be to make money in selling real estate. The way you achieve this goal and become capable of making money is the result of a three-way job.

First, get legitimate listings from owners who are ready and willing to sell their properties at fair market prices with agreements, signed by you, to sell. In other words, get exclusive listings.

Second, find a qualified buyer. This must be somebody who is interested in buying the property you have listed; who is financially able to buy the property, and who is willing to stop, look and listen to you.

Third, make the sale. Get the buyer and seller into an agreement with some cash in the hand.

Occasionally you will have a transaction in which the buyer refuses to give you a cash deposit, or something of value. It is your job to make the buyer understand that there can not be an enforceable contract if there is no consideration. So you must have a cognovit note or cash each time you make a contract.

Similarly, you can not hope to be a successful real estate salesman without desire; without the expenditure of time and effort.

Knowledge is the tool that will add to your success in the real estate profession. I honestly believe that you can not do better than you know how or what to do. And this is a real problem for the real estate salesman who frequently is called upon by the public, or by his own broker, to do something in which he has received little or no instruction. So, knowledge is what you need.

I will completely train you within the scope of this book. I will give you the knowledge and techniques and I will delve into the fundamentals that comprise salesmanship. In short, you will get all of the tools you need to do the job. I will help you to determine how to plan your attack so that you will know who to see, what property to show, when, where and why!

Indeed, after you are finished with this text, you will discover that you will be completely scheduled· able to know when, where, why and everything else about being at the right place and at the right time.

You will be unflinchingly convinced, as I am, that you must have good working habits to create real estate sales. This ability to create is the difference between a good real estate man or a failure. You are going to learn how to develop good working habits and how to gain control of the sales situation in the next chapter.

You will need enthusiasm, conviction and a deep-seated longing for success, too. But let me repeat, you can not do any better than you know how to do.

Your enthusiasm will be determined by your knowledge of the job. In fact, your survival in real estate depends on your ability to act as a true professional—one who can and will solve the other person's problems. For example, your buyer must move, get into a school district, buy in a price range, or get shelter. Your ability to solve such problems not only helps the individual buyer, but also gives you confidence and enthusiasm and molds your successful future.

Your survival depends upon this ability to help others. While you are engrossed in satisfying your own company, you have to recognize that there are people competing against you. If there is some phase of the real estate business which you don't understand and won't learn, it could bring about a fast exit in this extremely competitive world. Does that sound trite? Then consider these figures from the state of California: approximately 25,000 salesmen enter the real estate business annually in the Golden State while more than 20,000 others drop out due to their inability to make a living wage!

Be ready by having the right attitude and by knowing your job. Realize that half of the people in real estate are unable to make a decent living because of poor training. Make your goal success.

If you presently are selling real estate, you already know that you are your own success or failure. This book will give you additional knowledge and show you how to make personal improvements. It is up to you to apply the proven methods. It will be hard work, but if you understand our system, I promise that you will double your sales in the next six months.

Many of you will be a hundred, two hundred, three hundred times as great simply because these are the fundamentals you need to be successful in real estate—to make annually $16,000 or more in handling sales of real property.

Experienced sales persons have the added responsibility of unlearning erroneous sales theories and bad habits while simultaneously concentrating upon grasping the Rybka Method for Successful Selling. There is no doubt that it is easier to learn the right procedure the first time. That is a basic reason why this book is being exposed to the general public and, of course, to all potential real estate salesmen.

Please remember that the difference between success and failure is not in finding new tricks. The winner always is the one who is better trained and who knows all of the fundamentals. Consider the baseball teams as they go into spring training. I am quite sure that championship teams are not planning to learn anything new about baseball in spring training. Nevertheless, they emphasize the fundamentals so that their in-season play will be practiced, flawless precision.

This is what I offer to you who are presently in real estate sales. Better training in the more successful methods. You are going to have a lot of challengers intruding in your field. They will try to take sales away from you and it will be a battle. You never can say that you are the only one who understands selling. Lots of intelligent, trained people will be competing with you, so it will be wise to master this book and emerge as a winner.

You know the fundamentals are important. You have the right attitude and the desire to earn $16,000 or more a year selling real estate.

Let's get on with the "Know!"

Chapter Two

Plan Your Success with a System

In selling real estate there are five specific things which must be done:

1. Get exclusive listings from owner-sellers.
2. Inspect homes.
3. Show homes.
4. Make contacts with your bird dogs.
5. Sell something.

You can put all of the above into motion by making five cold canvasses a day, but you will need persistence and determination. Talent won't do it and genius won't do it.

Exhibits 2-1 and 2-2 are dramatic examples of telephone canvassing techniques that work

Plan an early arrival at the office. That means before 9 a.m.—and it should become a habit. It is proven that your best work hours, psychologically, are prior to noon; that your most restful sleep is before midnight. So adopt these natural habits as your successful work habits.

The ability to use your time wisely can depend upon how you discipline yourself with a preplanned schedule of activities. An outline for such a schedule is shown in Exhibit 2-3.

QUICKIE TERMINOLOGY FOR CANVASSING BY TELEPHONE

"Hello!

"Mr. Sherman, this is Mr. Edwards of Goodhome Realty.

"Mr. Sherman, I wonder if you can help me. I have a young couple with three children and $8,000 in cash. This couple would like to buy a home in your area. Do you know of anyone in that vicinity who is thinking of selling?

"Thank you for being nice to me, Mr. Sherman, and if you hear of anyone who might soon be selling, please call me, Mr. Edwards at Goodhome Realty, 587-3707."

RECOMMENDED TERMINOLOGY FOR TELEPHONE CANVASSING

"Is this (Mr. or Mrs.) Sherman?

"This is Tom Edwards, the real estate man.

"I have a serious problem. I recently sold a home for a young couple in the Heights area and from the sale of their home, they received $10,000 cash.

"The young man is a young executive with the Bell Telephone Co., and he has a lovely family with two children, Laurie, 10, and Jimmy, 6.

"I've been showing them homes in Clifton Woods and Park-view and have been trying to discourage them from living in your section, because I don't have enough available homes there. But they are asking for a home in your area because they would like their children to attend St. Jude School and Church.

"I took the liberty of calling you in hopes that you may know of friends or neighbors who are thinking of selling their homes, so that we may help this couple.

"If you hear of anybody selling their home would you call me, Tom Edwards, at Goodhome Realty?

"Thank you, (Mr. or Mrs.) Sherman, for being nice to me."

****

ALWAYS USE A BONA FIDE BUYER, TRYING TO SOLVE A REAL PROBLEM!

Exhibit 2-3

PLAN YOUR SUCCESS WITH A SYSTEM

It's your time! Use it wisely!

A. Listing volume and sales volume go hand-in-hand. Listing volume can be controlled if it is a PLANNED EFFORT.

B. Listings fall in three categories.
1. Call in. This type is the result of past effort. SOLD signs. Many "For Sale" signs indicate a successful organization. The "Sold" sign is conducive to securing good listings.
2. Listings are the result of personal calls, PTA, clubs, etc.
3. Listings one pursues. An added plus to your business. Volume in this phase depends on skill. One develops skill by practicing; by trying.

C. A typical daily plan for success follows this pattern:
1. Screen all newspapers for potential listings.   8:30 a.m.
2. Take various routes to office, looking for all possible listings.   8:45 a.m.
3. At office: answer calls; bring your listing book up to date.   9:00 a.m.
4. Call owners who advertise in your quest for listings.   9:30 a.m.
5. Scan daily legal news for blanket mortgages, foreclosures, etc.   9:45 a.m.
6. Call owners whose listings soon will expire with your company, as well as others whose listings have expired with other companies. Prepare mailing pieces.   10:00 a.m.

Variations in the foregoing time plan will occur, but the schedule above illustrates the general pattern.

A DAILY PLAN SHOULD INCLUDE THE FOLLOWING "MUST."

This is the absolute minimum! The greater the effort extended, the more successful one will be.

THREE OF EACH IS THE MINIMUM.

Three calls on buyers—you will receive prospects from buyers and you keep in contact for repeat business.

Three calls on sellers—both for contact and to have listing price adjustments.

Three "cold" calls on the telephone—you often secure listings
or prospective buyers. Remember, it is the exposure that
counts. The best article will not be sold unless people know
of it. Let them know you and your company.

Three "cold" calls at the door. This gives a similar result to the
above. You have the opportunity to show the occupant the
high type of person you are and you build client confidence
which is conducive to later contact if and when the
occasion arises for him to buy or sell. You have a much
better opportunity for having made the contact.

A Note to the Wife!

As a real estate salesman's wife you must remind your husband that
the above program if followed, assures your family an above-
average income commensurate with efforts expended.

Your office desk is your own work area. This is where you
operate. Whether you will be using a telephone, ringing a door
bell, or just looking for merchandise, you can initiate your five
daily cold-canvass calls from this command post.

Systematize Daily Activities

You will be shaping your own destiny. There are no time
clocks in a real estate office, so you must cultivate your own
good work habits. Analyze and know yourself and what you
need to do to improve. Capitalize on your strong points and
de-emphasize your weaknesses.

In selling, be systematic also. Follow a work schedule. Use
your bird dogs and maintain 10 to 15 active exclusive listings.
In a recent survey, over 50% of the former buyers said they
would not do business again with the same salesman. Don't let
them say that about you.

Being in the right place at the right time can be guaranteed
with the mastering of time. Or to put it another way, time is on
your side the moment you organize it. Exhibit 2-4 presents a
workable method of developing better work habits by keeping a
running tally of production progress.

Exhibit 2-4

A SCHEDULE TO PROGRAM
BETTER WORK HABITS

DATE: _____   GOALS: Listings _____
NAME: _____   SALES _____
                                           Reductions _____

NOTE: *GOLF* on *FREE* DAYS or back by *NOON!*

TODAY'S INTENTIONS:	TODAY'S REALITY:
8:30 ARRIVE AT OFFICE	8:30
Secretarial—Gum labels—mailings Know/Choose your Neighbor letters	
9:00 Work Folders—Appraisal Slips MLS Update—changes—Solds	9:00
9:30 Pictures Read Realty Section Advertisements	9:30
10:00 Ride FARM—Hit "by owners"	10:00
:30 Inspect listings—ours—MLS Pick-up SOLD SIGNS—Place signs	:30
11:00 "SHOW HOMES" or 5 FARM CALLS	11:00
:30 " " " " "	:30
12:00	12:00
:30 LUNCH—CHORES	:30
1:00 GO HOME	1:00
:30 " "	:30
2:00 "SHOW HOMES" or Inspect New listings on Teletype	2:00
:30 Call "old" clients—5 FARM CALLS	:30
3:00 Call your listing—report to Seller	3:00
:30 Tickler File calls—Bird Dogs	:30
4:00	4:00
:30	:30
5:00 DINNER HOUR	5:00
:30 Go HOME—CHORES	:30
6:00	6:00
:30 "SHOW HOMES" 1st Appointment or	:30
7:00 Present Work Folder Buyer/Seller Act Hit "by owner" at door 5 FARM CALLS	7:00
:30 Call Clients for TOMORROW SHOWINGS "SHOW HOMES" 2nd Appointment or	:30
8:00 set up closings of seller Get the listing signed	8:00
8:30 Set up next day's schedule Most Important things to do	8:30
9:00 GO HOME EXCEPT FOR CLOSINGS AND LISTING APPOINTMENTS	9:00

Build a clientele by staying on the side of the party you are dealing with, whether it is buyer or seller. You must be flexible and make the public understand that you are working in their behalf. Make a friend or booster in each sale by showing the buyer or seller that you understand his wants and needs.

Develop a Clientele

You don't sell a prospect a home and then forget about him—nor let him forget about you! This is so important because you are not in the business for only one, two or three years, but you will be selling all your life. The friends you make in one transaction will be working for you, calling you and saying, "I have somebody who wants to buy a home. Please sell them one because you're my real estate man."

You can reward these friends, too. Take them to dinner, buy them an electric can opener, or some good whiskey. Every time they use your gift they can say, "My real estate man bought me this." One of our salesmen found it advantageous to give a United States Savings Bond to the youngest child in his customer's family. The bond stays in the home and the gift is never forgotten.

If you have a good butcher, barber, cleaner, or insurance man, you are happy to make a referral. That is how you want people to think of you. Be a good real estate man! Get them talking about you and you will find that selling will become easier every year.

Sell Yourself

Selling yourself doesn't mean what it seems to imply. Actually, it calls for the most subtle form of salesmanship because you never can brag or boast about yourself to attract customers. If people like to deal with you, it indicates that they like you better than the next fellow; that you have gained their good will, confidence and friendship. You have indeed sold yourself.

People will want to deal with you if you have a pleasant personality and a satisfactory knowledge of good, practical human relations. How do you develop that personality? Rid yourself of negative habits. Develop positive qualities—and smile! The man who keeps smiling inspires a feeling of comaraderie and keeps the friendly attention of his clients.

As a matter of personal hygiene, be cautious of any obnoxious odors. Persons who smoke cigars, cigarettes and pipes should rely on breath sweetners. The aroma of tobacco often makes one's breath offensive rather than kissing sweet.

Consider your car, too. Many people are impressed with expensive cars. Frequently when taking prospects to see homes, they would ask, "Is this an Olds 98?" I was amazed at the number of people who were impressed by my car. Often they would add, "I wish I had a 98. You must be making a lot of money." I would reply, "Well, I am able to help a lot of people."

I heard such comments much more with the Olds than with my former Pontiac. I am not selling Oldsmobiles. I merely want you to realize that your car is important. If you must economize, don't do it with the car which can very well be the status symbol for the successful, professional salesman.

Put your best foot forward. Remember you are in the real estate business. Look like a businessman. Dress like one. Use that clean, late model, four-door car and watch your driving. You want the customer to be relaxed, feeling at ease in comfortable surroundings as well as with you, his considerate, interested friend.

Always strive to do something for your prospect. If you are to be successful in real estate sales, you have to feel sorry for the person who does not buy a home from you, because you know you have something good and he can not see it. Your zeal will be something like that of the clergyman who preaches against sin and feels sorry for the person who can't or won't get the message. You, too, must have this missionary spirit, recognizing that you want to sell homes because you are determined to help people.

Forget your failures! When you make a sale, try to discover why you made it. Was it because you handled the customer properly? Was it just your natural talent? Or was it tremendous salesmanship—of doing the right thing at the right time?

Even a star quarterback has to sit on the bench occasionally and analyze what makes a successful play. But if he, or you, spend bench time fretting about failures then certainly a bad mental attitude and self-defeating depression are due. Develop a buddy system with a friend in your realty firm. Daily, the two of you should discuss and exchange your successes, worries and problems.

Selling real estate demands tremendous courage. Experts tell us that most acts of heroism are the result of the individual's training and conditioning. The man who "chickens out" may not necessarily lack courage, but may be engulfed in a feeling of insecurity. Therefore, communicate your feelings to a friend. It will give you strength to face your next test and to put your convictions into action. Each time you succeed, the next sales task is made easier.

Slumps

If enthusiasm is lacking and a slump is pending, you are getting worse rather than better. Quick! Make more calls! Only by trying to help others can you help yourself. When you are selling, everything is fine. When things go bad and you feel like taking it out on your wife and your children, give yourself a pep talk and start making more calls. Repeat to yourself daily: "I'm good! I'm good! I'm going to make one more call; make many more calls!"

Professional baseball players have their slumps. Do they retire early? No. They go out with a bat boy or coach and hit balls for hours. Again, in golf, if it is a slice or hook that is bothering you, you don't play less golf. You practice and work at it more. You can shunt slumps by making yourself work harder.

The progress checklist shown in Exhibit 2-5 is an effective guard against sales slumps.

Failure to inspect homes and to know your merchandise also will cause slumps. Let me cite an example:

Our salesman showed a prospective buyer a home on Skyline Drive. Later, because of conflicting appointments, he

---

Exhibit 2-5

THE SLUMP BUSTER

SALESPERSON:_____ DATE:_____

PLANNED ACTION!! = $ $ $

8:30 a.m. PEP TALK!!   GOAL REVIEWED!   HIT THE ROAD!

MOST IMPORTANT THINGS TO DO TODAY:

1. _____ 4. _____
2. _____ 5. _____
3. _____ 6. _____

CHECK OFF YOUR PROGRESS, *NOW!!*

Visited   ) *Press*
Owner "Ads") *Bugle* 1. _____2. _____3. _____
5 Telephone Canvass 1. ____2. ____3. ____4. ____5. _____
5 Doorbell Canvass 1. ____2. ____3. ____4. ____5. _____
5 Inspect Listings
  or re-inspect   1. ____2. ____3. ____4. ____5. _____
Call Former Clients 1. ____2. ____3. ____4. ____5. _____
Showings   1. ____2. ____3. ____4. ____5. _____

Planned:
TOMORROW'S ACTION _____
_____
_____
_____

PLAN TO GET RICH THIS YEAR!

---

asked me, "Can you show this home a second time? The prospect is thinking of buying it."

I met the prospect and showed him the home again.

"I am going to offer $26,000 for this property," he said.

"Why?" I asked, judging it to be a low offer.

'Because ABC Realty has one for $26,000 and it is a new home and of the same construction as this one."

I did not know anything about ABC's house and I should

have known what my competitors' listings were as well as my own. I had no knowledge if one home was smaller or larger than the other, but I tried to hedge a bit by saying:

"Well, the homes aren't exactly the same. This home has draperies, carpeting, landscaping and is complete."

"So does the other home," the prospect snapped and with that, he "closed" me. I agreed to present his much-too-low offer and blew the sale. Instead of my closing the sale, he had closed me. And I knew it! I had violated one of the cardinal principles of our business; that of entering into a discussion with a customer without proper preparation—without becoming fully familiar, not only with our own merchandise, but also with that of our competitors.

An informed real estate salesman would have known all about his competition. As I sat there listening to this prospect tell me about my competitor's house, I said to myself, "You really are out of this ballgame." There was no opportunity for me to close. All I did was to get an offer signed and make a poor attempt at selling.

It happens to many experienced salesmen, but they won't admit it. In fact, I have seen this terrible error of not knowing the merchandise all too often.

In the case above, I later learned that there could be no true comparison between our listing and the home offered by the ABC Co. Ours was built on contract, not a project home. It was larger and had more top-cost features than the competitor's home. I was not capable of handling the prospect because I just did not know the merchandise.

So avoid slump-inducing failures by inspecting all the listings and by learning what your competitors have to offer. This knowledge is a prime tool in your sales kit.

Two important factors in real estate sales are:

1. Truth.
2. Listings.

There is nothing that you can say to the seller or buyer that will hurt your deal so long as you tell the truth. Nothing!

As an example, let me tell you about a home that was for sale for $35,000. The seller wanted to hold out when I presented a $32,000 offer. He asked:

"Do you think real estate still is going up in price, or do you think we've reached the top?"

"I think real estate still is going up and I think in the next few years it'll go even higher," I replied.

"Well, then I'll hold out for $35,000," he countered.

"Look," said I, "The house is too big for you. Your wife can't keep up with the housework. Do you really want to suffer with it for another five years in the hopes of getting two or three thousand dollars more? Why not sell it now and get the smaller home that you want and need. Remember, if we are in an inflationary market—and I think we are—the smaller home will also go up in value and price, so you won't get hurt by buying one now."

He saw the logic in these remarks and accepted the offer. Later he said, "When I asked you about the future of real estate I realized we are in an inflationary market, but I thought if you painted a black picture, I wouldn't deal with you at any price. I appreciate the fact that you told the truth."

The truth paid off. Incidentally, that seller sent us other customers.

I maintain that even small white lies should be avoided in real estate. You can't remember the fabricated stories and they often come back to haunt you.

Send Brochures

"Know Your Neighbor" brochures are beneficial when used correctly. When you sell a home, send 10 brochures to the neighbors. It is a goodwill gesture and it lets them know that you are proud to have added this newcomer to their neighborhood.

Exhibit 2-6 is an example of an introductory letter used by a Rybka real estate salesman.

The important thing about all brochures is that they should be followed with a phone call or personal visit. You don't consider your brochure to be junk mail and you know that you should never make a phone call without a reason. So let your brochure be your entry to another home and another prospect with a call that begins with this inquiry:

"Did you receive my brochure?"

Exhibit 2-6

LETTER OF INTRODUCTION

FROM THE DESK OF –

Ron Forbes   **RYBKA**
5085 Turney Road   **REALTY, INC.**
Garfield Hts., Ohio 44125

Tel. Off. 587-3700
   Res. 398-4095

    I have just had the pleasure of assisting Mr. & Mrs. Roy Roberts purchase the home at 8138 Holland Road, previously owned by the Jamieson family.

    It will be months before they are really settled; nevertheless, they will be delighted to welcome all neighbors who wish to drop in and get acquainted.

    My association with the Roberts Family has been most pleasant, and I hope this note will be the means of establishing a warm and lasting friendship among nice neighbors.

                    Very Truly Yours,
                    Ron Forbes

RF/bf

    You will get a "yes" response and the start of a conversation which can provide you with information for a future sale.

Become Known!

    Buy some postal cards, address them and give them to your mailman and milkman, saying: "I know you are on the route and can't get to a phone. When you see a lead, please jot it on one of these cards and drop it in a mailbox."

You can get your name before the public only through exposure. Become a precinct committeeman. Get elected to your church council. Volunteer as an usher. Join clubs and charity drives. Let your youngsters join the Boy Scouts and Girl Scouts and take an interest in their activities. Become active in baseball's Little League.

When you participate in your community, you become known.

Speak Correctly

Speak properly. Poor grammar often annoys persons who do not speak correctly themselves. You can improve yourself by reading some books on English composition.

Never use profanity in a sales talk. A cuss word always is a poor substitute for the right word.

What does this have to do with making sales? You could be relying too much on the major points of your sales and listing techniques and overlooking these minor points which can make or break a sale.

Furthermore, never discard selling points, examples, or testimonials just because you are tired of them. To the listener, they are new ideas.

Be relaxed and calm, not overly eager for a sale. Go a step farther, if you can, but do it honestly. Make the house seem hard to get.

But let's not be too relaxed. I am thinking of the salesman who feels he has to sit at his desk until the walk-in prospect approaches him and says, "We are looking for a home." Greet the customer, won't you? When a person walks in and you are doing floor duty, go up to him and shake his hand. Be pleasant while you determine how you can be of assistance. At this moment you are like a maître d' with the duty of greeting and escorting the customer and making him feel at ease.

Also, when you have such floor duty, police your desks. Throw the newspapers away, empty the ashtrays and put the phone books inside the desks when you leave. It should look like a business office and not a paper factory.

WANT TO BE A FAILURE?*

A bad attitude helps tremendously in getting you off to a poor start. A bad attitude will let you rest on your laurels even though you don't have any laurels at the beginning of your sales career. All you need be able to do is to read and write, drive a car, pass the license examination, have two references and no prison record.

You also have no record of accomplishment in other sales work, but selling is a snap, so plunge right in and go after the sale. No need to go at it full-time. You'll make lots of money in your spare time.

Naturally you need something to sell. Most bosses are stingy with their listings, so off you go to get a listing. Here the wrong approach is your best bet. Either be a know-it-all, or be abject in your pleas for the listing. Either attitude will destroy any tendency on the part of the seller to build confidence in you. If you take the know-it-all approach, sweep through the house criticizing the construction and the arrangements. Speed is important. Take no more than five minutes from basement to attic.

Now you are ready for the real head-on clash with the seller.

In the event that you get the listing in spite of yourself, the procedure should be something like this: Rush back to the office and put a small, colorless ad in the paper. No use writing good advertising—it might bring more calls.

At last you have a call. Here is the perfect technique for flubbing a chance to make a sale. Talk, talk, talk! Give the caller the smallest details about the house. Give him the address. Build him up for a letdown. Don't ask who he is, or if he is able to buy. Just wade in and give your all. In this way you can lose your chance for an appointment and you won't have to bother showing the house (he probably wasn't interested anyway).

In case the customer insists on seeing the house, don't bother to pick him up. Ask him to meet you there. Here's a real clincher: Be late! Then you're off to a bad start for sure.

Rush him through the house and if he shows any interest, ignore it and keep talking. Another sure-fire idea: take his attention away from the house. Bring up miscellaneous subjects such as religion, politics, or any other controversial subject that you might

---

*Excerpt from the pamphlet: *How to Be a Successful Failure in Real Estate,* by Realtor Clarice Giddings; published by Women's Council of Oklahoma City Board of Realtors, 1956.

think about. Tell him how to rebuild or redecorate according to good taste—your taste. Be vague about the cost of such changes. In fact, be vague about all facts and figures. If the buyer persists in wanting definite facts and figures, pick a few out of the air, but don't coddle him. Just give him enough to shut him up. Some people can be so tedious!

Of course a few setbacks can be expected. Should the prospect say he wants to buy the house, you'll have to go through the motions of writing a contract. It is a golden opportunity to show off your ignorance. A contract offers numerous chances to make mistakes and create misunderstandings. Omit a few important conditions entirely. Tuck in some misleading information. Make a few ambiguous statements.

Don't worry about the deposit. Take anything you can get. A dollar or less. Then he can back out when he changes his mind—and he will.

Now that one is out the window. You've made a giant step toward being a successful failure. Just keep telling yourself that success is only a matter of time.

Chapter Three

Let the Listing Be Your Gibraltar

THE FOUNDATION FOR THE REAL ESTATE INDUSTRY IS THE LISTING

Definition of a Listing: An agency relationship is created when one person agrees to act for another in some business enterprise. The person for whom the work is to be done is the principal and the other is the agent. It thus becomes the duty of the agent to work for the benefit of his principal and not to personally profit from this relationship, except for the right to be paid for the services he has rendered.

If you don't like the real estate salesman's typical seven-day work week with its long hours, become a listing specialist. Then you can work on a five-day basis, starting and stopping each day when you wish.

Pick a 20-block area and become as familiar with it as the mailman who handles that route. Statistics show that the average home changes hands every five years. In a 20-block area, 80 to 100 homes will be sold annually with commissions totaling $80,000 to $100,000. Your share, at the usual listing commission, will be $16,000 a year. Your fellow salesmen will say that it is a decent income for practically part-time work.

The most important sales factor in a listing is not the price,

44

but the reason for the sale. When you know the reason behind the listing you have a valuable tool to attract and sway various buyers.

Some typical circumstances which provide listings:

1. A new baby has arrived and the home no longer is adequate.
2. Owner has been promoted. Wants a home or address with more prestige.
3. Owner is being transferred by his company.
4. Death in family.
5. Children have married and moved away. Home is too big.

Consistently read your local legal newspaper, study sale-by-owner advertisements and cultivate friends among local businessmen or trades people. All are sources of listings.

Also, talk to the sellers of the property you already have listed. They probably had tried to sell their own property. A little chat may lead to good prospects for sales or additional listings.

When you see a sale-by-owner ad, quickly visit the seller, give him a ballpoint pen or some other appropriate momento and introduce yourself. Tell him a mutual friend told you that the home is for sale. If he should tell you he wants to try to sell the house himself, don't argue! Here is how I would handle it:

"Fine, but if you change your mind, I represent Rybka Realty and I think we are good because we have sold 70% of the homes we have listed within 60 days.

"Any one of the 43 experienced salesmen we have in our seven offices can sell your home. Further, we are a member of the Multiple Listing Exchange and all of its 40 cooperating brokers and their combined sales staffs would be at your service, offering you prompt, experienced, reliable service."

At about this point the seller usually invites the listing salesman into the home. It gives the salesman an opportunity to make a favorable comment about the home and to ask questions which will serve him in good stead later.

"Such a lovely home and a fine neighborhood! Why are you selling it?"

If the reason stated is a transfer, or the purchase of another home on a blanket mortgage, recognize that here is a home that must be listed and sold. The pressure is really on the seller.

I think the reason for selling is far more important than the so-called "asking price."

Recently, I talked to a man about listing his home. He said he had no reason for selling; that he wanted $23,000 for the home. In my opinion, the home was worth $18,000. I rejected the listing. If he had been on a blanket mortgage, I would have taken the listing, waiting until later to show him his true position.

Often a prospective customer will ask, "How much do you think my home is worth?"

My suggested reply: "Well, I see your home has a lot of extras. It wouldn't be fair to you if I simply pulled a figure out of the air. There is so much in your home that, truthfully, I can't give you an accurate figure because I might be low on my appraisal. When you are ready to list, we'll sit down and put a value on everything you have in the house. Everything, so you don't undersell!"

With such a reply you have a suitable answer to the request for a free appraisal.

Saving the Commission

Frequently, a seller will say, "I'm going to sell the house myself and save the commission. Why should I pay you 7%? If I sell it myself I can afford to take $1000 less for the home."

Answer the objection this way:

"It is possible, but remember, a lot of buyers know you are trying to save a commission and they will try to cut your price.

"Many times I can get more for a home just by finding the right buyer who will pay the top dollar. The buyer who would fit your home, for instance, would be willing to pay a little extra.

"And though it may appear on the surface that you are paying the commission, actually, it is the buyer who pays the commission."

Two to Tango; Three to List

Perhaps in your listing talk you only have been addressing your remarks to the seller's wife and she is ready to tell you, "We'll think about it." Thank her. Tell her if they decide to list to remember you. Then leave!

You must plan a followup meeting in which you can present your story to both the husband and the wife. It usually is impossible to tell which one is the dominant personality. One or the other could swing the listing to you, or away from you. To be on the safe side, you should strive to "sell" both of them.

Should you go back to see the husband? What excuse can you use to go back? You MUST go back, even though it is a hard thing to do. This is where most real estate men fail. Seldom is a listing made on the first call. You must return frequently, check on their lack of progress in making a sale and assure the sellers that your company can do the job faster and easier.

Your return call might go something like this:

"Mr. Jones, I am Don Emerson of Seltzer Realty. I talked to your wife earlier. I know that you are selling your home and I'd like to know who you are and get better acquainted."

Jones: "We are going to try to sell it ourselves for awhile. We're not in any hurry."

Emerson: "Fine, but if you ever decide to use a broker, you'll find that we have the experience and contacts so that we can get the financing for the buyer of your home. Of course, when you are trying to sell your own home, you really don't know if a prospective buyer is qualified, or if he has enough money.

"Maybe the prospect has a lot of bills, or his credit is bad. Usually a buyer is wishy-washy and doesn't like to reveal this personal information, particularly to the other principal in a transaction.

"On the other hand, prospects that come to our office, come for consultation and advice. They tell us how much money they have for a down payment and they want to know what they can afford to buy and what their payments and interest rates will be.

"This knowledge of terms, of knowing where to get financing, or the most favorable mortgage and interest rates, can mean all the difference in making a sale. We have this in our favor when we are selling your house because we have the bank contacts. We are professionals who are trained for this business.

"Also, buyers like to make comparisons. They don't buy the first home they see. So after they have inspected your home, you can't take them to other houses and point out the most significant comparative details. We can, and in this way we can prove to the buyer that your home is worth the price."

Jones: "Well, I don't like to tie myself down. I'll let you have this place on an open listing."

Emerson: "Some brokers work on open listings. They're desperate and will work on anything. Of course they aren't going to spend any money advertising your house. They'll work on their exclusives first and do something with yours as a last resort. All of the brokers you can line up to work, half heartedly, on an open listing won't do the job as well as one broker who has an exclusive basis to concentrate on the sale of your home.

"The man with the exclusive knows from day to day what is happening to your listing, how to cope with every issue and how to adjust his efforts to fit one of his prospects into the home you are offering."

Jones: "But what if you don't sell my home?"

Emerson: "Our batting average is nine out of ten. We are not perfect, but most people are satisfied with our service. Once in awhile we get a knock, but usually it is from a person who is telling a slightly distorted story, ignoring the fact that he was demanding a few thousand dollars too much for his property. A seller's unreasonable attitude about his home's value probably is the biggest reason in failing to make a sale.

"Let me point out that a seller usually has too many obstacles to overcome in making a sale. When a prospect telephones, the seller has no alternative but to give the address and price, even before he knows who is calling him. We can throw the caller off guard and get information from him without revealing all of the details about our listing.

"We know, for example, that a $17,900 buyer frequently

settles for a $19,500 home to satisfy his needs. We must elevate the buyer to a higher price range. You, as an independent seller, haven't the experience or background to convince the buyer that he can move up.

"Furthermore, even if your house is priced properly and the offer you have received isn't too low, you'll have the normal legal difficulties and red tape to worry about. I don't even worry about them myself. We have our legal department and escrow department to solve problems and expedite the paper-work. You probably would lose quite a few days running around town trying to take care of these details, wouldn't you?"

As the clincher, I often tell the story about the seller who told me he would let me list his house if he couldn't sell it within a week. The following week he met me at the door and told me he had sold it. I congratulated him and departed. Two weeks later he called me, asking me to come and list his house.

"What happened?" I asked.

"I thought I had it sold," he replied. "I had wanted $16,500, but when this fellow saw the house and offered me $15,500, I reasoned that I wouldn't be paying a commission, so I agreed and we made a verbal agreement to go to the bank for an application. Two days later when we met with escrow officer at the bank, the buyer says he had talked it over with his wife and would only pay $15,000. I got angry and left. At home, my wife convinced me it would be silly to waste time looking for another buyer; to accept the $15,000. So we made another appointment, went back to the bank, and—wouldn't you know it—this time the buyer says he'll only pay me $14,500."

I not only listed that house, but also, I sold it to the same buyer—and the price was $16,000!

So You're Ready to List!

When the seller agrees to let you list his home, don't bluntly ask him how much he wants for the property. Strive, instead, to get him to voluntarily suggest the price he really wants.

Don't argue about his price! The secret is to get sufficient time to sell the home. As you make your weekly reports after getting the listing, there will be ample time to present logical reasons for a price adjustment.

If the seller is being completely unrealistic about his price and appears determined to stick with it, don't ridicule him. It is better to observe: "It is a nice home. Very nice. But I'll tell you the truth. I want to be honest. I don't think I can sell your home so I wish you a lot of luck."

Although you don't intend to take the listing, there is no reason to create an enemy. Perhaps you can do business with or through this owner at some future date. And in the real estate field, you always can use a friend.

In listing, be professional. Don't be the lister that says, "Give me your house today; I've got a buyer to look at it tonight," or "Give me this house and we'll advertise it six times a week." Don't lie.

The listing should be recognized as a two-way agreement. The seller offers the promise of certain things to the broker. The broker offers to be the sales manager; to advertise the home in a way that will get the phones to ring; to notify all cooperating brokers.

You are saying, in effect, we will be partners and as soon as you sign this listing form, I will set the machinery in motion so you can take advantage of our special sales campaign. Tell the customer you are not just a lister; that behind you there is an entire battery of salesmen, appraisers, closers, advertising specialists ready to work for him. Make sure that he knows and understands that many people, grouped together as a company, will work for him once the agency contract is signed.

When the seller decides to let you list his home, I recommend that you measure the house, its foundation and its rooms. If you do this meticulously and demonstrate that you have a formula, it is the type of showmanship that will impress your customer.

The more thorough you are, the more your customer will respect you and be ready to heed your advice later when it might be necessary to argue for a price adjustment.

I say you won't know what a house is worth until you appraise it. If you try to appraise it without measuring it or

estimating its reproduction cost, you are not qualified to bring
in the listing because you don't know its value.

A real estate man kids himself when he says he can tell
what a house is worth just by looking at it. You may not want
to tell your seller your appraised price, but you should have the
appraisal information if you are going to talk intelligently and
convincingly.

Nevertheless, the good real estate salesman must know
how to meet changing situations as they occur—in other words,
to play it by ear. He will realize that the greatest benefit of the
appraisal method is showmanship.

He must know, too, that an appraisal is only an estimate of
value with a spread of possibly $500 or $600 either way. He
also must know the three approaches to an appraisal—the
income approach, the cost of reproduction and the comparable
sales approach.

The important thing is to use the appraisal to impress. If I
were the seller, I know I wouldn't want a bunch of real estate
salesmen who merely look at the stars and then give me opinion
values. I would want to feel confident that the salesman
estimates the price for my house as accurately and profes-
sionally as possible.

At our company we say all listings should be calculated for
listing price and the company "sold book" should be used for
verification. The "sold book" consists of data about all the sales
we have negotiated. It gives an alphabetical address listing of the
properties, stating when the homes were sold, name of buyer
and the price. With this information, our salesmen can compare
prices for similar properties on a given street.

Here is our formula for figuring reproduction of bungalows
and colonials, up to 20 years old, in excellent condition:

Bungalow		*Colonial*
FDN. 30 x 30 = 900 sq. ft.	900	FDN. 22 x 24 = 528 1st floor
x cost per sq. ft.	$19	528 2nd floor
	8100	1056 sq. ft.
	900	Cost: $15 per sq. ft.
Cost of home:	$17,100	$15,840

If the property has been neglected, estimate the cost of fixing it Also depreciate the property one-half per cent per year.

Here are some other estimated values we use in making appraisals:

Lots: estimate value at $150 per front foot.
Storms & screens: aluminum—$600; redwood—$400.
Garage: 1½-car—$1500; 2-car—$2000.
Upstairs: one room—$1500; two rooms—$1800.
Recreation room: $1200.
Porches: $800 each.
Add 10% for brick.
Less: $400 for decorating.

Exhibit 3-1 is a sample appraisal form which is suitable for all listings.

The appraisal includes the commission. The reproduction includes the commission figure. How do you justify this? In the same way that a doctor justifies his fee—by making the customer feel that you have earned and deserve the commission. You save the customer money by having the proper connections to get him the most economical financing. You free him of legal entanglements and expedite all steps of the transaction from offer, through escrow, to possession and distribution of funds.

Again, these are some of the same reasons you will be using to convince the seller that it is you who should be permitted to list his home.

In summation, I recommend that salesmen keep the following listing aids in their personal manuals.

SUCCESSFUL APPROACHES TO GETTING LISTINGS

DO NOT refer to EXCLUSIVE LISTING, but rather use the term:

CONTRACT OF EMPLOYMENT or AGENCY CONTRACT!

Approaches to use in talking to sellers:
1. EDUCATIONAL: Tell seller how a house is sold.
2. SERVICE: Explain that we handle all the details.

Exhibit 3-1

**APPRAISAL FORM FOR
ALL LISTINGS**

MEASURE FOUNDATION

```
                          _____
                          _____ FOUNDATION SIZE
   X $_____per sq. ft.   _____

                          _____
                     $_____ Cost of Home
ADD Value of Lot     $_____
GARAGES              $_____
EXTRAS:  BEDRM. Up   $_____
     REC. ROOM       $_____
     STORMS/SCREENS  $_____
     PORCHES         $_____
     ETC.            $_____
                     $_____
                     $_____ Cost of Home, NEW
                     $_____ Less Decorating
                     $_____
                     $_____ Less Deprec., if any
                     $_____ LISTING PRICE
```

3 COMPARABLES–Recent Sales, or Sold Book
   ADDRESS:_____
      PRICE: $_____
   ADDRESS:_____
      PRICE: $_____
   ADDRESS:_____
      PRICE: $_____

3. PROFESSIONAL: Buyers prefer to deal with an experienced agent.
4. COOPERATION: Stress cooperation between brokers to sell quickly.
5. CONFIDENTIAL: Some sales require secrecy and tact.
6. SPEED: Transferred sellers; keep the family together.

7. NEGOTIATION: We negotiate higher prices from low offers.

8. HONESTY and REPUTATION: We belong to all the realty boards and our reputation is more important than any one deal.

9. ONE PRICE: If open listings are permitted, the various brokers may quote different prices and cause confusion.

10. ADVERTISING: Owner has only one property, but we have several; advertising does not sell, it only brings attention.

11. MARKET: If seller is optimistic about sales market, agree; if he is pessimistic, all the more reason he needs a broker.

12. FINANCING: We have good connections, but owner has none.

13. MARKET ANALYSIS: Show seller he is in competition with all other properties.

14. VALUATION: Sales price is seller's responsibility; broker advises, but does not dictate.

15. LEGAL: We avoid legal pitfalls for seller.

16. COSTS: We keep costs to a minimum for the seller.

17. YOUR AGENT: We represent and protect the seller against sharp buyers.

18. EXPERT SALESMEN: Selling is our job. We are experts.

19. BACKLOG OF BUYERS: Tell seller we have lists of buyers looking for specific properties.

20. SPECIAL SALES FEATURES: We have sales contests and pay bonuses.

21. PHYSICAL: We use signs and distribute pictures.

22. EXPOSURE: We are in the business of exposing houses to buyers.

BE LOGICAL IN THE USE OF THESE APPROACHES
STRESS BENEFITS TO THE SELLER

LISTINGS

Sources of Listings:

1. Owner signs and ads.

2. Referrals from satisfied customers.
3. Personal zone of influence (clubs, church, acquaintances).
4. Natural causes—births, deaths, marriages, promotions.

Types of Sellers:

1. Must sell.
2. Wants to sell.
3. Willing to sell.

In Your Visit to the Seller You Must Build Confidence in:

1. What you say and how you say it.
2. Establish mutual connection—either an acquaintance or a neighbor whose home you recently have sold.
3. Compliment property.
4. Write notes as you inspect.
5. Knowledge of neighborhood.
6. There are three important factors in the value of a home:
   a. location
   b. location   LOCATION IS 90% OF VALUE!
   c. location

In Your Visit to the Home, Find Out:

1. Who is the boss.
2. How long they have lived there.
3. How much they paid for it.
4. Why they are moving. The REAL reason!

Value:

1. Price the listing after you are hired.
2. Give Market Value figures, not appraisals.
3. Comparison of surrounding houses is best method.
4. Get a complete listing of all pertinent facts regarding property.
5. Title evidence.

6. Have office staff inspect.
7. Notify neighbors of availability because they may have friends interested in living in the area.
8. Service the Listing by Frequent Visits and Calls!
9. Use the word HOUSE when talking to the seller.
10. Use the work HOME when talking to the buyer.
11. Get Price Adjustments–Not Price Reductions!

Chapter Four

Eye Your Listings Knowingly

Real estate is a fantastic business because there always are new experiences to dispel monotony.

However, the least interesting aspect of real estate for the majority of sales personnel, I am afraid, is the task of inspecting homes.

It probably also is true that the reason salesmen don't like to inspect houses is because quite commonly the homes are overpriced. If the price is expected to become a barrier to a future sale, the salesman is less anxious to spend any time with that particular property.

I would remind you that you must follow the rules which are basic to everyday life if you are going to be successful in real estate. One such rule—and it is a great rule of selling—is to know your property, or product.

If you don't know your listings, you won't be able to sell them. Furthermore, your competitors will be making you angry because they will be making sales simply because they know your listings better than you do.

Listing knowledge is important. It adds sincerity to your sales talk. In contrast, we had a salesman who decided to show a house we had just listed to a potential buyer. He did not inspect the property. He merely checked the information on the listing card and guessed that the house would have a standard floor plan. So he made an appointment with his customer and took her to see the house. Upon escorting her into the kitchen, the salesman said, "And here, Mrs. Pinckny, I want to show you what a big, beautiful walk-in closet we have." With that, he opened the door leading to the basement.

Did his action show sincerity? Did he convince the buyer that he was qualified to sell the property?

Here is another incident. When I was a salesman, we had a vacant home across the street from our office. We had a six-month listing on the property and I had heard our salesmen describe it as a "dog" and complain that it was overpriced. I did not bother to inspect it because I knew what two-story colonials are like. They are all the same, right?

Finally, one day I walked into this house and inspected it carefully. Only then did I realize what a tremendous value it represented. I sold it and my buyers still are living there.

One reason I sold that house is that I was the only one in our office who had walked across the street to look at it. The listing came in through an attorney and we erected our "for sale" sign, but no one bothered to go inside the house.

That is what happens in real estate. Don't inspect the listings and the buyers quickly realize that you don't know what you are talking about. They lose confidence in you and lose interest in the transaction. But don't try to visit too many homes in one day. That is a good way to get house indigestion.

Restrict yourself to the activities of residential districts in which you feel that you will be able to sell the most homes. Go down the street and inspect every house that is for sale. See the properties, meet the owners and talk with them. The need for a friendly relationship with a client is a prerequisite for successful selling.

Schedule Visits

Schedule your appointments to inspect properties. You do not have the time to waste going to residences where people are not at home. It is better to make a phone call and let the owner know you are coming. Tell him he doesn't have to doll up the house; that you are not bringing anybody with you.

If the asking price is high and seems to scare you away, remind yourself that there also is a market place and a time for adjustment. Frequently a salesman will walk into the house with a $19,300 price tag and immediately recognize that it only is a $16,900 house. If that happens to you, don't let it sour your thinking about the property.

Remember, the reason for selling a home is more important than the price. If the sellers are serious about selling, they will take offers from qualified buyers and sell at the market price.

Inspecting the Listing

It always is best to go alone when you make your intitial inspection of a newly-listed property. When salesmen go in groups, they tend to distort each other's opinions. An inconsequential comment about the price, floor plan or neighborhood can lead to a general affirmation that it is a poor listing and that the property has major flaws.

When company policy dictates that salesmen will go in a body to visit each new listing, return to the property later and inspect it again alone. This is a must! A seller will talk to a salesman with much more candor when he is alone, rather than when the salesman is in the midst of a group.

When is the best time to inspect a new listing? Just as soon as possible. There is nothing more impressive to a seller who has just signed an exclusive listing contract than to hear the doorbell ring and find that another salesman from the same company is anxious to inspect the house.

"The lister was just here," the owner will say.

"I know, but I am here to inspect the property and see if I can find a buyer for it," you reply.

That really gets the seller enthused. He knows your company is working in earnest for him.

Explain to the owner how hard you will work for him and make certain that he knows that all of the facilities of your experienced, efficient real estate company are at his disposal.

You really should spend 30 to 40 minutes inspecting each listing. Again, it will impress the seller and make him happy and proud that he has assigned the listing to the right company—your company.

If you have tried hard to win the friendship and respect of that owner, he, in turn, may try to be a little nicer to you by giving you some good leads. These will be about prospects who he knows are thinking about selling their homes.

Other chance remarks can help, too. Upon stopping to inspect a newly-listed home, I made a pointed effort to compliment the owner on her choice of decorations and furnishings. The house was tagged at approximately $5000 more than the market price, but as our friendly conversation continued, the owner confided that her husband would accept less money. Although she was not ready to admit it to the public or to our other salesmen, she said she would take $2500 less. Three hours later I sold that home and listed the buyer's house which I also sold the same evening.

Indeed, it pays to inspect listings alone; to take the time to get acquainted with the seller and to search for sales clues. You should spend 20 to 30 hours each week inspecting homes. It may seem like a lot of time, but it must be done if you want to know your merchandise and to make sales. Our most successful listers advise us to make all inspections in the morning. They tell us to restrict our inspections to two or three listings per day. To that, I would suggest that if you have no new listings to check, spend your inspection time rechecking the homes you already have seen. You will find that frequently you will have a different opinion of what those homes are like. The return trips could remind you of new prospective buyers who will fit into those houses.

As you walk through a property, you must retain an accurate mental picture of what the house is like. You are the professional shopper for your prospective buyers and it will be advantageous to take notes concerning the most significant features of the property.

You must attempt to juggle two sets of facts; facts about the property you are inspecting and facts about your prospects who are looking for homes. Your job is to match the physical characteristics of the house in question with the known wants and desires of one or more specific buyers.

But why should you spend so much time in inspecting listings? It is primarily to absorb the environment of the home. With a thorough knowledge of both the buyer's and the seller's environments, selling becomes a simple task of matching up people for other people's homes.

We make it a point to call each of our listings weekly to reassure the owners that we are trying our hardest to find buyers. Most sellers do not expect miracles, but they do expect to be kept well informed, even if progress has been slow. It is most discouraging to me to note that even active, high-caliber real estate men frequently abuse this privilege of providing thoughtful service.

The seller wants to know if there has been any action on his house. Tell him! Say, for example, "There is an abundance of work done at the office answering calls on your home. We are getting a lot of inquiries from low-down-payment prospects. Some of these people have stopped at the office, offering a ridiculous price and since we are your legal agents, we have declined the low, marginal offers.

"Basically, this matter of selling your home is a team effort. And at this time, we have all members of our staff participating in the manhunt for the right buyer."

As you meet with your sellers weekly, it will be easier to reach a mutual agreement on the most salable price. He will be more receptive to your counseling when you explain that the longer a home stays on the market, the less he will receive. Once he understands the logic of that fact he will be more amenable to your suggestion that the price should be adjusted. Again, in giving weekly service, you are strengthening your future position with that customer.

Industry-wise, most listings expire. But if you were thoughtful enough to write a thank-you note to the owner when you received the listing and if you contacted him at least weekly thereafter, the chances are that you will be able to renew that listing. And on the second time around, you will begin on the premise that the job is half done.

In this latter "grace period" you already are acquainted

with the property and your customer, so most of your time can be spent in concentrated, productive effort.

Adjusting the Price

A salesman asked me when it would be safe to ask the seller to lower his price. I maintain that it is not enough to list the property, but after taking the pains to evaluate it, contact the seller frequently for an adjustment of the price.

If you ask for an adjustment within a week, the seller still is in the mood of doing so. Don't wait a month, two months or three months to seek a price adjustment. Do it immediately! It sometimes is helpful to call the owner when you have returned to your office right after listing his home, saying, "Our real estate men who have sold thousands of homes tell me this price is wrong. What should we do?"

Later, you might want to say to this same owner, "A few days ago, I discussed your lovely home with other brokers and colleagues. They asked me what decision you made regarding your selling price."

Such a comment opens the door. It takes you off the spot and puts the seller on it. In effect, you are needling the owner because it is your responsibility to let him know the true market value of his property. So you must needle your seller to adjust the price to a range in which a prospect will buy and the seller will do what he desires—sell his home.

Still later, you might say, "Mr. Gordon, I have been standing in front of your home trying to figure out what is wrong. Can you help me? Do you think it is the price?" This approach will give you repeat business and make your sellers satisfied. Sellers don't expect miracles, but they do expect courtesy and care.

You should be careful, though, that the owner understands that you are relating what somebody else has said; that it is not your own opinion.

It is never "I" who thinks the price is too high. It is "they." Make sure it is "they," "the public," "other brokers tell us the price is ..."

Then, if the seller explodes and says, "Well, come and get

your sign," you can add, "I'm with you. I told those brokers they're wrong. I am going to keep on working hard to help you."

Never be caught making yourself the authority. If you can always place yourself on the side of the seller, "It is us against the world," he will listen to your advice.

A telephone call can be extremely helpful in getting a price reduction. Here is how we put such a call to work:

"This is your real estate man calling.

"Are you getting any action on your house? Has anyone shown your home lately?

"Is our sign in front in good condition (if you have a sign on the property)?

"How about the price? I discussed your house at our weekly meeting with the other salesmen and the other brokers. They are complaining that the price is too high. What do you think? Of course, you are my boss and I will do anything you say. I am reporting to you what the others are saying. But what do you think? If we had a full cash buyer today, what is the lowest price you would take?"

(The first one to speak loses!)

"Let's adjust the price to the true figure you want so that we aren't discouraging buyers with our phony price, O.K.?"

If that comment fails, say: "I will call you again next week to keep you informed about what is happening in the sale of your home. In the meantime, if you think of any other ideas, call me immediately."

When the price is adjusted, say: "Thank you for the adjustment. I will put it on our teletype immediately so that all of our seven offices will know that we have a new price to quote to our buyers. Thank you, Mr. Gordon. This new price can make a world of difference in the action for your home."

Chapter Five

Attracting Buyers
with Bright Ads

In real estate sales, the biggest expense item is advertising. Our company, for instance, spends about $4000 a month on advertising. That is quite a bit of money and yet it is an expenditure that represents a sound investment.

Why? Because advertising is your introduction to the world of success. Your ads should be designed as carefully as the colorful jackets for best-selling books. They must make a favorable impression and emphasize the desirability of the product.

It is not the purpose of this book to teach a course in advertising, but there are some general rules or guides with which you should be acquainted.

Keep in mind that in creating a favorable impression, good ads make it easier to get those much-desired listings. Of course, the immediate and most important result of a good ad is to produce qualified lookers who can be converted into buyers by knowledgeable salesmen.

All too often, real estate brokers and salesmen are overly concerned about the cost of advertising, but foolishly waste most of their advertising dollars. In their typical classified advertisement they try to cram in too much detail. They minimize or ignore the heading and make their name or signature too large. As a result, the reader's eye is not attracted to the body of the ad. A large signature has never sold a home, but emotional headings and tempting copy can and do create desire and lead to sales.

A few examples of how Rybka Realty's daily classified advertisements attract interested prospects are seen in Exhibit 5-1.* Note how they follow all of the recommendations covered above. Typical home sale advertisements in *The Cleveland Press* show that Rybka Realty makes effective use of white space. In

Exhibit 5-1

SAMPLE CLASSIFIED ADVERTISEMENT

HUNTING THIS SEASON?

Set your sites on this large wooded 80x180 ft. lot with a practically new 3-b e d r o o m ranch, 1½ baths, desired family room, wall to wall carpeting, d i n i n g room, patio, at-t a c h e d 2-car garage. NEAR SCHOOLS. 3571.

RYBKA REALTY, INC.
895 E. 222nd   261-6300

HAND-PICKED . . .

Split level setting on grounds 160x225 ft. Modern k i t c h e n with b u i l t - i n s, dishwasher, wall-to-wall carpeting, formal dining room, DEN could be 4th bedroom, 2 full ceramic baths, covered patio off family room which is enhanced by a brick wall fireplace, full basement, a t t a c h e d 2½-car garage. ·ONLY 5 years new! Brecks-ville school system. 09277.

RYBKA REALTY INC.
6510 Brecksville   524-3660

PICTURE WINDOW FACES . . .

Park g i v i n g the wall-to-wall carpeted living room of this young ranch a beautiful scenic view! Formal dining room, 3 b e d r o o m s, kitchen-dinette, dishwasher, w a l k -o u t base-ment with rec room, attached double garage. Split rail fence enhances the 75x173 ft. lot. Mid $30's.!

RYBKA REALTY INC.
5489 Ridge   886-0470

*Reprinted with the permission of *The Cleveland Press*, 901 Lakeside Ave., Cleveland, Ohio.

contrast to some of its fellow advertisers, the Rybka Company's ads have interesting headlines with an emotional appeal. The body copy tells some, but not all, of the details of the individual property that is offered and the signature (which does not really sell a house) is held to a conservative level.

The number of homes you advertise daily will depend upon the number of exclusive listings your firm has. However, if your ad contains more than one house, run each property separately with an individual signature. This will allow all your listings to be read as individual offerings.

You should realize that sale-by-owner ads are well read. Also, many of the new real estate firms use small ads with success. Unfortunately, when some of these firms grow, they abandon the small ads and use large box ads with expensive artwork and big signatures.

It would be better to use the money spent on art and big signatures to advertise additional homes for sale.

All good ads—ones that produce many phone calls—should be filed in a folder containing examples of successful ads. These can be designated as good pullers and can be repeated when needed.

In our own Rybka Realty scrapbook, we have many successful ads which we re-use time and time again as the occasion warrants. Here are some examples:

RACE FOR SPACE?

Not in this large three-bedroom bungalow with modern kitchen, dining room, living room, full basement and gas heat. And because it is brick, upkeep is at a minimum. $25,900.

HAY FEVER SUFFERERS

The only thing you can sneeze at in this large 3-bedroom bungalow is the low price. Newly installed central air conditioning will give you summer-long comfort. New carpeting, 2 clay tile baths, divided basement. $21,900.

WALK OUT . . .

To the enclosed patio from the paneled family room in this luxurious, 4-year-old, 7-room brick ranch and view the lovely grounds. Test your skills in the modern kitchen. Carpeting, formal dining room, recreation room with bar, attached 2-car garage. $34,900.

RESTFUL VIEW

From the screened-in porch overlooking a lush, wooded ravine teeming with wild birds. This view will be yours in this lovely 2-bedroom bungalow; clay tile bath, expansion up; attached garage. Only $20,500.

FOR SWING & SLIDE SET

"Cause this comfortable 6-room single is on a "dead end" street—SAFE! Tiled bath, 3 bedrooms, built-ins. Awnings. Possession before school opens. $22,900.

GONE FISHIN'

To the sparkling lake on the 5 acres surrounding this peaceful brick ranch, of meticulous construction. It has 3 bedrooms, 1½ ceramic tile baths, formal dining room, the magic of a family room with log-burning fireplace, plus basement recreation room and novel kitchen built-ins.

Tomorrow Is Too Late!

PLAY IT COOL

In this air-conditioned master brick ranch. One of the four bedrooms is 34x15 feet! Electric built-in kitchen, formal dining room, first-floor utility room and 2½ baths means it is designed for the modern large family.

Service Beyond the Contract

_____

FOR BEGINNERS

In a good location, this 5½-room bungalow is only $13,300. It has living and dining rooms, large kitchen for informal entertaining, two bedrooms and full basement.

Open Sunday, 2-5; Daily, 9-9

_____

WANT SECLUSION?

This brick ranch is so picturesque you must see it to believe it! Luxuriously carpeted and draped living room is enhanced by an open hearth; hospitality beckons you to the formal dining room; well-arranged kitchen, tiled bath; 2 bedrooms, possible 3rd up; library, den, paneled rec room, jalousied sun porch, attached 2-car garage. Picnic area on the 5½ acres.

Big. . . .And. . . .Friendly

_____

INVEST—DON'T SPEND

Is what you'll be doing with this well-kept 2-family, 4-4. Two bedrooms, modernized kitchen, carpeting in each suite. Full basement, 2 gas furnaces, double decker porches. 2 garages. St. Stan Parish.

14 Years of Fair Dealing!

_____

A SPECK OF DUST

Would die of loneliness in this delightful 3-bedroom bungalow; carpeted living room, large kitchen with corner sink, full basement, gas heat, garage. Southbury school district. $23,500.

Over 7600 Homes Sold in 14 Years

_____

After a realty company is established it should consider the use of institutional ads which will create a fine company image.

Exhibit 5-2* is an example of an institutional advertisement that will build sales while it boosts the company's image.

Most broker ads can be improved with the use of larger, bolder headlines, smaller signatures and sufficient white space on the sides and at the top and bottom. Done this way, the ads will be easier to read and easier to identify.

We made this simple test. We placed a one-column, two-inch advertisement in our local newspaper for a test run. Then we took this same ad and added 20% more white space. Upon running it again we found that with the white space it brought three times more response.

Now certainly there are practical, economical limits as to how much white space you will want to use. You probably won't want to double or triple the size of an ad merely for the sake of adding white space. However, you should indent your lines of body copy or add a line of white to the top and bottom of the ad to make it more attractive.

Many prospects have told us that they contacted us because they liked the looks of our advertisements in the evening newspaper. Achieving such attention is an invaluable assistance to any broker, especially when you consider that house hunters frequently turn to the classified advertising section before they even read the news headlines in the same paper.

Currently, the eye stopper in our ads is a weekly sales thermometer in a diagonal position. Before we began to use the thermometer, our ads were practically the same as the majority of realty ads in the paper. Now, though, we have a more attractive ad with more white space and more eye appeal. In reporting the sales achieved each week to a general market, we actually are pre-selling a future market of buyers.

A typical institutional advertisement for Rybka Realty, as shown in Exhibit 5-3, sells the value of trading and graphically illustrates the company's sales progress.

---

*Reprinted with the permission of *The Cleveland Press,* 901 Lakeside Ave., Cleveland, Ohio.

Exhibit 5-2

INSTITUTIONAL ADVERTISEMENT
THAT BUILDS SALES

THANKS TO YOU!!

OUR DADDIES DID IT AGAIN!

Our Daddies reached their "6–" goal in 49 weeks! Buying or selling, see our Daddies, they will work hard to make you happy, too! Please call them at any of the 5 Rybka Realty offices today!

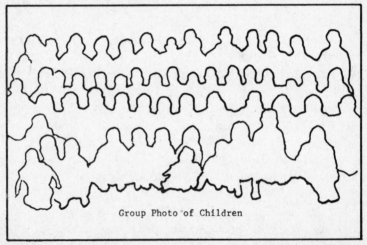

Group Photo of Children

| VU 3-0370 | DI 1-3400 | GR 5-0300 | TU 6-0470 | LA 4-3660 |
| 9812 Garfield Blvd. | 6310 Fleet Ave. | 5244 Warrensville Ctr. | 5489 Ridge Rd. | 6510 Brecksville Rd. |

REALTOR **(RYBKA)** 5 OFFICES

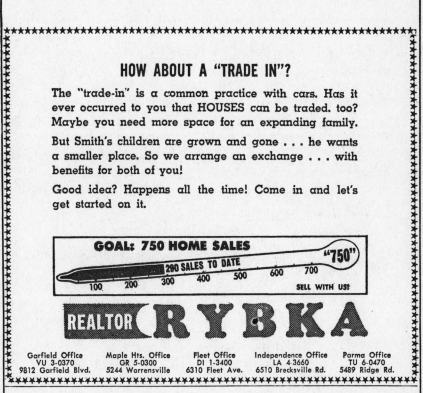

Exhibit 5-3

INSTITUTIONAL AD THAT SELLS THE VALUE OF TRADING

In composing your ads, realize that you are in the highest-paying profession in the world. Realize, too, that there is an entirely new crop of buyers coming into the market each day. Therefore, advertise daily and write ads that will get people to act—to call you.

Professional advertising people have written books on the do's and don'ts of copy writing, but I think the ones you should concentrate upon in composing real estate advertising can be condensed into these statements:

● *Do* talk directly to the prospect in your headline and body copy. The word "you" can't be overused. Be natural and friendly in conveying your message. Make the reader want to live in your house.

● *Do* be honest, for it makes your ad believable and wins confidence for your firm.

● *Don't* promise things to the prospect that aren't in the house you are advertising.

● *Don't* talk in negatives or use stereotyped phrases. There always is something good about every house.

● *Do* name the benefits—the many aspects of the house and your company that are desirable.

● *Don't* follow the others. The true result-getter is that which you have and which no one else can advertise.

● *Do* an adequate job of describing the home and the buyer you are looking for.

● *Don't* be afraid of long copy. People read every word of an ad that appeals to them and descriptive copy creates such appeal.

● *Do* tell the prospect to act promptly and make it easy for him to do it. Give your name, address and phone number (he may not be able to make it that day, but he might be interested in the property anyway).

● *Don't* mention the name of a salesman to see or call if he or she won't be available to show the house or to give the prospect more information.

● *Do* repeat ads that created above-average response.

● *Don't* repeat ads that brought limited response.

● *Do* use a consistent advertising program during the week. Each day has its market.

● *Do* spend time with your advertising for it is the most valuable time you will spend.

You want the reader to stop and read your particular advertisement, so stop him with an emotional heading. People buy their homes emotionally and in using the emotional heading, you will find that you are getting calls in direct response to your appeal.

The so-called screwball heading also is a stopper, but often it will not invoke the type of interest in your home which you desire.

Make it a rule never to copy your competitors' headings. Also, avoid using trite headings such as "Owner Says Sell," or "Make Offer." Instead, be alert to good headlines or headline ideas as you browse through *Life, Look, Better Homes & Gardens,* or any other popular periodicals.

You will find self-interest headlines usually are based on an outstanding feature or advantage of the home and can be in the form of a statement or question, such as:

Big Family Wanted	Room to Breathe
Like to Entertain?	A Place to Relax
Gardener's Paradise	Looking for Value?
5 Minutes to Freeway	Away from Traffic
Close to Schools	Prestige Neighborhood
A Home of Distinction	Adventure in Space

Informative headlines such as "3-Bedroom Ranch," "8 Rooms," and "Brick Bungalow," while they may have appeal, lack the interest of more imaginative headlines.

Curiosity headlines also will fall flat if they bear no relation to the readers' interests. To be effective, the curiosity headline must have human interest and emotional appeal. Here are some good examples:

Hurry! Hurry!	Congratulations
Lucky You	Dream Come True
Love at First Site	Guess What
Happy Days	Newlyweds
Undecided?	I Kid You Not
You'll Be Surprised	Oops!

At the end of this chapter, I have included a list of prime examples of emotional headlines. I always keep such a list at my fingertips. I recommend that you do, too.

The body of the ad need not be long if the heading is attractive.

In advertising a home, pick an outstanding feature or two and mention but little more. You could note features such as the architectural style, the approximate location, lot size, number of rooms, unusual room sizes, number of baths, playroom, den, patio, extraordinary landscaping, transportation, schools, churches, or shopping facilities.

Generally, you will not mention such items as venetian blinds, dishwasher, garbage disposer, and incinerator. Don't give so much detail that you create reasons for your reader to reject the home sight unseen. The secret of good advertising is to give just enough information to arouse the prospect's interest and curiosity. And, as I stated earlier, not giving sufficient information also can lose sales.

It is interesting to know what home buyers are looking for and what advertisers are telling them. A comparison was made about two years ago and reported by *The Cleveland Press.* * Here is what the survey disclosed:

WHAT HOME BUYERS LOOK FOR:		WHAT MOST ADS TELL THEM:
Price and Terms	75%	67%
Number of Bedrooms	66%	84%
Size of Lot	65%	19%
Square Footage	48%	4%
Convenient to Schools	47%	24%
Convenient to Churches	46%	9%
Number of Closets	41%	1%
Garage	40%	60%
Convenient to Shopping	38%	9%
Built-in Items	34%	22%
Convenient to Busline	28%	5%

In conducting an advertising program in which you are describing many homes each day, you will experience difficulty in being creative or in maintaining originality. Again, the national magazines will be an important source of ideas inasmuch as the advertising contained therein has been prepared by the advertising men who are in the top echelon of their profession.

---

*Reprinted with the permission of *The Cleveland Press,* 901 Lakeside Ave., Cleveland, Ohio.

With sufficient care in the preparation of your advertising there is no doubt that your telephone will begin to ring. Once those calls start to come, it will be up to you. You must learn good telephone procedure, or lose a percentage of your good prospects.

According to the advertising experts, if you don't have the budget to run attractive, more costly ads, run fewer ads. They will be the ones that will push up your sales volume, not your advertising bill.

Here are a few brief rules to make even the budget-attuned ads do a husky job:

1. Know the property. Inspect it thoroughly.
2. Determine who most likely will be your prospect.
3. Select the property's most appealing feature.
4. Allow yourself to get enthusiastic about the property.
5. Pick an outstanding heading.
6. Choose the words and the ideas that you believe will create the maximum desire for the property.
7. When advertising more than one home daily, appeal to as many buyers as possible by incorporating a selection of home styles. For example, a single day's offerings might include a colonial, bungalow, ranch, and an income bungalow.

A few pages back I mentioned *The Cleveland Press*. I do approximately 80% of my advertising in that evening newspaper, about 19.8% in the morning paper and only 0.2% in the Sunday paper. From time to time, *The Cleveland Press* uses these figures in recommending itself to other brokers and builders. A typical recent *Press* promotion letter read: "Rybka Sales Prove Value of *Press* Ads. . .Greater Cleveland brokers and builders who are looking for the secret of success would do well to study the methods of Edward F. Rybka, dynamic founder and president of Rybka Realty Inc. Setting a challenging sales goal at the start of each year, this enterprising organization has broken its own records each of the 14 years it has been in business."

Actually, *The Cleveland Press* has helped me to increase

home sales not only in the results that its advertising columns bring, but also with the many advertising tips it offers its advertisers. For example, the current *Press* ad-writer's brochure states:

"Successful real estate ads are written from the prospect's viewpoint. As you prepare an ad, ask yourself, will the ad attract the prospect's attention? Will the headline arouse his interest? Does the ad give sufficient information about the house to enable him to determine whether it meets his family's needs and desires? Does the ad make it easy for the prospect to reach you or to find the home?"

Buyers do not read every ad. They select those which attract their attention and appear the most interesting. So watch your layout. Break copy into paragraphs and separate ideas with white space. Use lower-case letters for body copy because they are easier to read than capital letters. Distinctive borders help, but the most effective border is a wide margin of white space.

Despite anything you may have heard elsewhere, the public is *not* your market. The public *contains* your market. You can not write an ad that will appeal to every prospect, so concentrate on those who are looking for the type of home you are offering. So be informative, specific and truthful.

Above all, don't neglect to romance your product. Let your body copy paint colorful word pictures. Big living room? Fireplace? Country kitchen?

No!

Better try these:

"Spacious living room designed for gracious entertaining."

"Contemporary fireplace that's a real conversation
piece."

"Country-sized kitchen makes cooking a pleasure."

Or, these expressions:

"Master bedroom with breeze-catching corner
windows."

"King-sized closets."

"Peach-colored tile bath with double sink."

"Cheery family room that invites 'togetherness.' "
Big shaded patio you can enjoy every hour of the
day."

Headline and body copy should stimulate the prospect's
interest, but don't keep him guessing. According to advertising
experts, the omission of the price of the house is a principal
reason for the failure of real estate ads to get results.

The experts say real estate ad writers omit the price
because they think this will induce the reader to call, or because
they are afraid to mention price until the prospect has seen the
house, or they hope to draw prospects for other homes that the
company has listed.

Although some brokers argue that the price should not be
stated in an ad (and indeed, there may be very sound reasons
for not using the price in some ads), the ad experts say that
much time, effort, and money are lost by real estate men in trying to trap prospects with price-less ads.

They contend that the prospect who suddenly finds he has
wasted time with a house he can't afford is generally soured on
the idea of looking at other homes offered by the same broker.
Also, while the buyer does watch his dollars carefully, it doesn't
necessarily mean that he is looking for the lowest price he can
get.

Prospects—and that includes all of us—want the best value
they can get for the price they can afford.

By stating the price in your ads, you will get more
quality-conscious prospects, fewer lookers and more qualified
buyers. Hence, more sales in quicker time.

I have found that real estate ads get their greatest reader-
ship in the evening. That is because most people work during
the daytime and are unable to relax with their daily newspaper
until nightfall.

But here is a word of caution about your ad in the
afternoon or evening newspaper. You might expect the prospect
to call the day after the ad appears, during your regular office
hours. However, if the prospect calls in the evening and gets no
answer, or if he is switched to an answering service that can not

supply detailed information, he will lose interest in your house and turn to another ad.

Make it easy for the prospect to reach you by putting into your ad both the numbers of your office and your home, plus the hours that calls will be received at those numbers. It might be helpful to include another salesman's number, too.

The day of the week is important, of course, but perhaps not as much as you now think. Each day, hundreds of families in every major metropolitan area start looking for a home for the first time. Unless your ads appear daily, you risk losing many of those prospects to other advertisers, including owners, whose ads appear on the days you skip.

It is true enough that innumerable home inspections are made on weekends, but it is the advertising on preceding days that builds up such activity. Many prospects who plan to look at homes during the weekend make their selections in advance. The broker or salesman who waits until the end of the week to advertise will lose some of those prospects who already have made their plans and appointments for the weekend.

Another reason for daily advertising is that newcomers to town create a persistent, steady need for thousands of homes annually. U. S. Census figures show, on the basis of a full year's study, that an average of 30 new families per day—more than 200 per week—move into my county alone.

Because of their urgent need, these transferred families are ideal prospects and the most likely candidates for quick home sales. Only through daily advertising can you be sure of reaching these prospects while they still are in the market.

Finally, let's switch back to the heading, remembering that the most important function of the ad is to catch the reader's attention and interest.

Let me re-emphasize that your heading should make an emotional appeal—perhaps even a low-keyed emotional appeal—to the prospect. With that in mind, I have assembled the following list of headings from a much more extensive list that we have available at Rybka Realty headquarters. As I said before, it would be a good idea to copy this list and add to it from time to time. You will be surprised how often such a handy list will inspire you to write a better advertisement.

HEADINGS

Hearts Are Young
Designed for You
Feel No Pain
Like Strolling?
Like Golf?
Enjoy Life More
Country Casual
Reflects Good Taste
Within Your Reach
Unlimited Potential
Find Relaxation
Garden Lovers Only
Beautiful Start
Something for Everyone
Try It, Today!
What Mom Wants
March in Before April
So Nice to
    Come Home to
Join the Rent Rebellion
Come Here Tonight
Get a Fresh Start
Needs Boys & Girls
Gentle Persuader
New Horizons
Tired of Compacts?
Dazzle of White
Snug Warmth
Gift to the Bride
All My Lady Wants
Cheery Childhood
Miniature Estate
Children Will Love It
Land of Lakes
A Sweet Deal
Be The Judge
Budget Stretcher
Without A Worry
Kid-Proof
She'll Thank You

Spectacular View!
Life Begins at 40!
Here's the Key
Love Beautiful Things
Add it All Up
Eliminate Maintenance
Touch of Elegance
The Country Scene
The Staying's Easy
Roomy Comfort
For Royal You!
Sheltered Location
Made to Order
First Class
Priced to Enjoy
House Too Tight?
Hey, Look Me Over
If Comfort Counts

Helps Your Future
Moving With Care
Look Once
Elected for Today
Wee Wonder
Let's Go Modern
It's Easy to Enjoy
Spending Is Good
For Men Only
For Active Living
Make a House a Home
Loll in A Pool
Paradise Found!
Count the Extras
Room to Grow
Why Deny Yourself?
Life Is Short
For Teeny Tiny Tots
Star Bright
Cherished Tomorrow
Extra Privacy

A Quiet Home
Garden of Ah's
Storage Space?
Lasting Warmth
Get Comfortable
Star Among Stars
Dining at Home
Be A Prince
It's Plush
Sunnyside
For Joyful Years
Feel Fall Snugly
Seven Pines
So Rich!
Cream and Sugar
CHIC for Chicks
On a Clear Day
Call It Charm

Dreamy Setting
Special Indeed
Improve Yourself
Look at This!
Scene Stealer
Well, Here 'Tis
Professional Size
Step Saver for Mom
Luxury Without Tax
Snug Haven
To Love In
Get Compliments
Right In Step
Wonderful World
Glowing Address
Fire-Safe, Too
A Yard Wide
Looks Lovelier
Entertaining More?
Treasure Chest
Stepping Stone

End the Space Race

More Space for $$$

Plus A Big Patio

Suit Yourself

You'll Love Living

Success Is Automatic

Key to Home

Mother's Gift

No Dark Corners

Sophisticated Lady

Good Taste? The Best!

Sincerely Yours

Swimming A-Go-Go

Your Private World

Forever Yours

Like Old Houses?

Bedrooms Open Outdoors

Practical Folks

Wide and Wonderful

Check Your Choice

Old, But More Fun

Bridal Sweet

You'll Feel Safe

Did You Know?

Imagine the Beauty

Dine In Style

Her Kitchen

Window Beauty

Invest in the Best

Source of Delight

Happiness Forever

Luxury Touch

Woman Appeal

Enduring Value

Show Off

Take Your Pick

Be Our Guest

Million Dollar Dream

Centerpiece of Beauty

Your Love Nest

American Love Call

Home Planning Center

Baths A-Plenty!

Fits Your Plans

Order Peace of Mind

Ideas In Action

Like to Entertain?

Golden Touch

Stunningly Styled

A Reason Why. . .

Season's Surprise

Escape the Ordinary

Best Years Are Now

Meant for You

When Company Comes

The Uncommon Touch

Takes In A Lake

Sturdy Look

Rich to the Eye

A Good Thing

Built for Loafing

Showcase Kitchen

Status Symbol

Tight Budget

Step-Saver

New As Tomorrow

Cold As a Barn?

Easy to Own

Dawn Buster

Greet Each Day

Envy of Neighborhood

The Right Answer

Gives You More

No Painting

Low Budget Economy

O.K. Mom!

Surprises Galore

Looks like $35,000

Help Yourself

Healthful Comfort

Graciously Yours

Fairest of All

Safe, Sound & Sweet

Use It With Pleasure

Settle for Less

Get A Lot, Too

Pleasing Approach

As You Like It

Graceful Styling

Features Prestige

Year-Round Comfort

Pamper Yourself

A Hot Box It Ain't

Think Pretty

You'll Love It Madly

Guests Encouraged

Point with Pride

Pearl of Little Price

Just Looks Expensive

True Family Friend

Worry Proof

Backyard Chefs

Eye Popper

One to Grow In

Why Look Longer?

Size This One Up

Be Warm As Toast

Preferred for Value

Ideas in Action

Like It? Then Look

New Horizon

Perfect Spot to Live

Have More Fun

Best Foot Forward

Security for You

The Eye Catcher

For Keeps

Smartest Move

Safety Planned

House Hunting?

Forever Sharp

So Easy to Own

Youthful Glow

Step Beyond Best

See What's New

Show It Proudly

Fill It With Friends
Congratulate Yourself
Mighty Safe Buy
Money Isn't Everything
Dare to Be Different
Happiness Lives Here
Something to Crow About
Once in a Wifetime
Open Your Door
For Lazier Living
Of Course You Can
Stops Traffic
Looks Little, Acts Big
For Busy You
New Executive
Sweeten Your Future
Intimate Hours
Consider the Facts
Extra Living Space
Designed for You
Fit for a Queen
Cradled in Love
Made for Each Other
Love at First Site
Cozy Den—Lucky You
Beats Rent Receipts

Halfway to Heaven
Made for Loving
Scheme A Little
Lifetime Protection
For Growing Children
Let's Be Practical
Fresh As Spring
Some Delightful Day
It's Party Proof
Outdoor Chefs
Feel Cramped?
Your Wife Should Know
Everything You Need
Always A Pleasure
Home of Enchantment
Poetically Pretty
Come Up and See
Heavenly Days
Living's More Fun
Professional Planning
Outlast Your Mortgage
Everyday Magic
Flatters Tender Budgets
Wallet Watcher
Home Sweet Castle
Sweeter than Suites

Cleans With Ease
Look Your Best
This Is Living
Pleasure to Spare
Place, Show & Win
For Easy Growing
Smart & Thrifty
Personally Yours
Young For Years
As You Like It
Comfort Zoned
For the Young Set
We're Neighborly
Your Good Taste
Warm Their Hearts
Neighbors Wanted
Irresistible!
Happy Haven Kitchen
Young Marrieds
Happily Ever After
Beauty Rooms
Midas Touch
New as Tomorrow
Hungry for Flowers
Joy Forever
Luxury Labeled

Chapter Six

Telephone Techniques That Generate Sales

In the last chapter I noted that once the calls begin coming, you must know telephone procedure. The greatest loss of revenue in any phase of the real estate business, to both salesman and broker, is poor telephone technique.

What happens is that you answer the phone and hear a prospect saying, in effect, "Tell me the price of the home you have advertised and I'll tell you my name and phone number if I am interested."

It is imperative that you know who you are talking to and refrain from giving any information until you know the name and phone number.

Tip No. 1—Guard the Address

What is the sense of advertising a property without an address if you are going to give that address to an unknown telephone caller? On the other hand, if the caller is a prospect who is interested in buying a property, he will not be ready to accept a weak excuse that you can't give him the address because of company policy.

Why can't you give an address over the phone? Let your

answer be that the seller does not want you to do so! Say to your caller:

"Friend, I'd like to give you the address. I'd love to, but the seller just called and said there are so many cars on his street that if I give anybody else the address, he isn't going to talk to me any more. I promised I would not."

Most likely, the caller will say, "Well, you can give the address to just one more person."

To that you can reply, "You want me to break my promise? Now please be nice. Okay? It's my word. Don't let me shatter it."

That takes you off the hook. The prospect does not care about any policy, but if your word has been given to keep an address secret, that is important.

Tip No. 2—Get Your Mind Into Gear Before You Talk

We all experience the same situations in handling telephone calls. We are writing an ad, planning a listing talk, addressing envelopes, or listening to the latest jokes. All of a sudden, the telephone rings and we are not quite ready for it. What to do? Take a deep breath for a second and get set mentally before you pick up the receiver. Then in a pleasant, unhurried way open the converstion by saying, "Rybka Realty. Mr. Walker speaking. May I help you?"

That first impression with a prospective buyer can not be minimized. Present yourself as a person who is informed, but do not attempt to act too erudite.

Tip No. 3—Get Them to Talk

When you tell each caller that you have five or six similar homes, some better values than the home advertised, you can get the caller to start talking about himself. Explain that in order to show homes that fit his needs, you must have some information. Get all the pertinent facts by asking questions and follow your prospect pad. Check off the type of buyer he is and what he needs.

When you have him talking, make an appointment to show him a house that will fit his needs. Ignore the house that initiated the call if it is apparent that it won't fit the prospect's needs. (Seldom will you sell the advertised house to a caller.)

All too often, a person who calls a real estate office actually is merely seeking information on how to buy their own home. They don't have any idea of what type of loan they can get, or what their monthly payments will be, so they hope that they can weasel such information from you. Don't educate them by telephone. If you do, they no longer will need you.

A better course of action is to learn something about your caller. How much can he pay down and what amount can he afford to pay monthly? It is embarrassing to ask a man how much he earns. If it is a very modest amount, he might be ashamed to tell you. If it is a sizable figure, he might be afraid to tell you for fear you will try to oversell him. So, via phone, inquire casually, "Out of your savings, how much money are you planning to use to buy a home?"

If he replies, "Five or six thousand dollars," he means he is ready to pay down $5000 to $6000, so why do you have to ask him how much he makes?

Tip No. 4—Qualify Him First

If the caller is sincerely interested in buying a home, he will answer your questions. But it is up to you to weed out the callers who are not serious buyers.

Take command of the situation by qualifying the prospect before he can qualify you. Be alert and prepared to act quickly. You must convince the caller to allow you to help him. Use your qualifying sheet. Check size of family, family's needs, earnings, etc. Get and keep this information.

A sample of such a sheet is shown in Exhibit 6-1.

The low-down-payment prospect may not offer you much opportunity for success, but be kind to him. Give him the same treatment you would give the "money" customer because today's low-down-payment client is tomorrow's qualified buyer.

Generally, the low-down-payment buyer, VA buyer or FHA buyer is a first-time buyer and easier to please and easier to sell. Once in awhile you will find such a buyer who will try

Exhibit 6-1

SAMPLE QUALIFYING SHEET
–TO HELP PRODUCE SALES

SRE #   №   3169
Prop. 2502

Buying Motive _Retarded Child Special School_

MUST HAVE:

Bedms 3	DR	Own X	Rent
Baths I	Bsmt X	No hurry	
Bunga I	Col	Must move X	
Ranch	2 Fam	Must sell first X	
Split	Gargs 2	Bills	
Const Frame	Age 20		
Bus X		Man X	Wife X
		Boys I	Girls I

SCHOOLS: Other

Public X

Parochial   PRICE RANGE $25,000

Special X   Down Pyt. $ 5,000

CALLED ON: Mo. Inc. $ 700.00

Sign____ W.I.____ Adv. X Other____

Phone # 883-9029

Name Joe Buyer

Address 4875 E. 95 St.

Employed Federal Savings   Phone 587-3707

Properties Shown

to dictate terms even though he is in no position to do so. You must tell him the terms and be firm.

Tip No. 5—Realize Why They Called

All too often a broker or salesman who created an appealing advertisement will get a telephone call and will forget what the appeal was that prompted the call.

Don't be misled into thinking that all of your callers are interested only in the house that was advertised. You used an emotional appeal in choosing the heading. Thus, the majority of persons who call will be seeking a state of life and not just the advertised house. Always be prepared to tell each caller about the other fine houses you have to show, some of which might even fit him better. If they responded to your appeal, you should have a fair idea of what they really are seeking in a home.

At this point, let us look at a demonstration of telephone technique in handling a "tough" inquiry.

(Telephone rings.)

Salesman: Home Realty. May I help you?

Buyer: I am calling about your ad in today's *Press.*

Salesman: I have six other similar homes that might fit you even better. Who is calling, please?

Buyer: Wait a minute. All I wanted was the address of the house. I just wanted to flash it.

Salesman: Well, would you hold on just a second, please. I don't have the information here. Hold on a minute. (Pause.) I don't have the ad here right now and I have to leave on an appointment. Could you give me your name and phone number and I'll buzz you right back with the information?

Buyer: Can't. I'm at work. In fact, I am calling from a pay phone and can't stay here. I have to get back to my machine. I just wanted the address so I could flash it on my way home.

Salesman: Hold on again. I'll talk to the manager. I'll see if he has any of the information.

Buyer: Fine. O.K.

Salesman: (After a short pause.) At the time we advertised this home, we picked out a few houses comparable to it, all similar, some better priced and with about the same layouts. If I may, I'd like to have your name and phone number so I can call you later at home. Either that, or as long as you are at work and it is going to take so much time to talk, I'll call your wife at home and give her the information on all of these homes so she will have a good idea of exactly what is available. What is your name and phone number?

Buyer: Here's the situation. Every time I give my name and phone number, I get a flood of calls and I'm not interested. They call me on colonials and I don't want colonials. This ad sounds like what I want and I wondered if you would give me the address. I just want to ride by it.

Salesman: Well, you see the seller of this particular home called and told us that there have been too many people riding past the house. The seller made us promise that we would not give the address to anybody else. So, give me your name and I'll call you, or should I call your wife?

Buyer: My name is Matthews. Tom Matthews.

Salesman: I see. Matthews. What's your phone number Mr. Matthews?

Buyer: It is 777-7777.

Salesman: Is that at work, or at home?

Buyer: It is my home number.

Salesman: All right. What is your phone number at work, or can I ever reach you there?

Buyer: No. This is like I said a public phone.

Salesman: O.K. Fine. By the way, Mr. Matthews, that name seems familiar. Do you have relatives in Cleveland?

Buyer: No. I am from West Virginia.

Salesman: Oh, I see. Do you own a home now?

Buyer: Yes, but we sold it. We had it about a year and a half and we sold it.

Salesman: Where is the home located?

Buyer: Right on Hazelwood.

Salesman: Right on Hazelwood. Then you plan to locate in the area here?

Buyer: Yes. I like Cleveland. I just need more room, that's all.

Salesman: Good. Do you have any children?

Buyer: Yes. I have two boys.

Salesman: I see. Are they attending the Maple Heights schools?

Buyer: One of them is, yes.

Salesman: Which school is that?

Buyer: It's Stafford.

Salesman: Stafford? That's fine because No. 4596 is in the Stafford area.

Buyer: Is that right?

Salesman: Yes, it certainly is.

Buyer: Well, how much is that home?

Salesman: That house is $16,900.

Buyer: That's a little too high. I didn't intend to pay that much.

Salesman: Well, you see, the important thing is if you like the house. Now this home that you are calling about would probably be perfect for you with your two boys. It has three bedrooms and a recreation room, a double garage and a dining room. It is a beautiful home. If you like it, I'll see if I can get it for you.

Buyer: Actually, I'm really not interested in a recreation room. If I have to pay the price for the rec room, this is just a little too high.

Salesman: That is all right. I have another home that is $15,900 and has the same qualifications, but no recreation room. What time are you off work?

Buyer: About 5:30.

Salesman: And how long does it take you to eat dinner?

Buyer: Well, if you want, I could meet you right after work.

Salesman: Better than that, what's your address? As long as you are in the neighborhood, I'll pick you up at 6:30.

Buyer: That would be all right, too, but I thought I'd save a little time and go to see it myself. Then if I like it, my wife could always come later.

Salesman: I'll call your wife. We will set an appointment and I'll pick her up at 6:30, too. That way you can save yourself an extra trip.

Buyer: That sounds pretty good. In fact, it sounds a little better.

Salesman: What is your address?

Buyer: 381 Hazelwood.

Salesman: On Hazelwood. Oh, yes, that's right. Mr. Matthews, I'll see you at 6:30.

Buyer: See you then.

Early in the telephone conversation the salesman should seek the caller's phone number. At that point, it is more important than learning the caller's name. When you ask the caller for his number it keeps him off balance and eliminates phony names. It is more difficult to give a phony number than a phony name.

The person who gives you his number promptly and without stammering must have one in front of him or in his mind, so you can assume you are talking to a legitimate, interested buyer.

Mention your name frequently. You want the caller to remember you if he has occasion to recall your office.

Look at the letter in Exhibit 6-2. Sending such a follow-up note to a recent phone caller pays big dividends.

One method we have used effectively to get a name and telephone number is to tell the caller: "We are getting a tremendous amount of action on that ad and the salesman is out showing the house now. He has all the information. If I can take your name and phone number, I'll call you back." Many times, the thought that other persons are looking at the house increases its desirability and makes the caller so excited, he will give his name.

As soon as I have the caller's name I ask, "Have you a pencil and paper?" Ninety-nine times out of a hundred he does. He is ready to write down all of the information.

I say, "My name is Ed Rybka." I spell it out for him. I add, "Now do you have our phone number? It is 587-3700." Then I ask, "What is your phone number?"

When a caller refuses to give his name or phone number, skip over that problem and continue to qualify him. Usually he will give some indication as to where he wants to live. At about that point, I will remark:

"Then you are looking for something off Washington Park Blvd. I am so glad that you called at this time because I was

---

Exhibit 6-2

SAMPLE FOLLOW-UP LETTER

Michael L. Fraser   **RYBKA**
5085 Turney Road   REALTY, INC.
Garfield Heights, Ohio 44125

Telephone: Off. 587-3700
        Res. 581-3398

Dear Friends:

Thank you for calling our Office. The selection of a new home is one of the most important decisions a person makes during his lifetime; and I sincerely desire to help you find exactly the home you want.

Our office has a broad selection of homes in the price range you mentioned, and new listings are received daily.

Since our Office has sold over 7,600 homes in the past fifteen (15) years, I know I will be able to serve you as well, in your search for a perfect home.

For your convenience we are open from 9 a.m. to 9 p.m. daily and Saturdays from 9 a.m. to 6 p.m.; our Sunday hours are from 2 p.m. to 5 p.m.

I would appreciate a telephone call, in advance of your visit, so that I can arrange to be in the Office at that time.

Remember, you always get *service* beyond the contract from *Rybka Realty, Inc.*

                              Sincerely yours,
                              Michael L. Fraser

MLF/fm

---

talking to one of our salesmen about 10 minutes ago. He told me that he received a call from an attorney who is handling an estate on Gamma Ave. You know where Gamma is, don't you? Right by the school? But there is a little problem. The attorney is taking care of probate work and it should be cleared up in five or six days. The home either is going to come in at the end of the week, or the first part of next week.

"From what the salesman tells me, it is a three-bedroom

bungalow. All on one floor. It has a front porch and I think he said aluminum siding. There is a full basement, new copper plumbing and a two-car garage. Our salesman appraised it for the attorney and he thinks this house will be sold for $11,900 or $12,900.

"Now this is going to be a hot listing and I am sure that the house will sell immediately. If I had your name and telephone number, you would be the first to know about it when the home comes in."

You will be surprised at how fast the caller will give you his name and phone number when you describe a future attractive buy.

Some Final Tips

Telephone conversation is so important! Brokers can make the telephones ring, but if you don't know what to do about the calls, you are helpless and the advertising money is a waste. You might just as well have been somewhere else.

When you are on the telephone and other lines start ringing, no matter what the conversation, immediately excuse yourself, saying, "Just a minute. Our phones are ringing. I'll be right back."

That lets the caller know there is action in your office. Also, if you stay with him, ignoring the second or third calls, you will lose one or two prospects whom you should corral.

In bouncing back and forth from one telephone conversation to another, you can tell your callers, "Everybody is calling about that house. Hear those phones ringing? Same home! I want you to be one of the first to see it, but I have three other people calling, so in order to clear our telephone lines, give me your number and I'll call you right back."

Another technique is to tell the caller: "The salesman in charge of that listing is on another telephone. May I have your phone number? I'll have him call you back in a few minutes."

Obviously, it is to your advantage if you can get the caller's number. Then there is not the danger of losing the call, or of being so rushed that you can not give each call the proper attention.

The telephone is vital to the success of a real estate salesman. Don't abuse it.

Chapter Seven

Your Buyer—To Know Him Is to Win Him Over

Everyone is aware of the fact that a salesman should know his product. But the real estate salesman also must know his buyer and his buyer's wants and needs.

It is here that most salesmen are sidetracked. Buyers will talk about their dreams, but the salesman must consider the size of the buyer's family, the amount of down payment that will be available and the neighborhood or environment which will be most acceptable. The salesman must reckon with facts, not dawdle in dreams.

Know Your Buyer's Goals

Visit the buyer's present home, realizing that people usually stay in the same environment. If the buyer is slovenly, he is not going to change his habits just because he is buying a new home.

Analyze his needs and desires and enter this information on a prospect file card where you won't forget it. The information should be put in writing because it might be days, weeks, or months before you successfully match the customer with a home.

Your goal is to show the buyer the house he needs and can afford to buy, meanwhile ignoring his expressed dream. The selection of a home, it has been said, can be compared to a girl falling in love. She forms the vision of a prince charming—a dashing cavalier with white horse and shining armor. But when you meet her one day and she introduces her future husband, it appears that knighthood and royalty were booted out the window.

Therefore, don't try to prejudge your prospect, nor guess at what he wants. To really qualify a person, you must see beyond his dreams. Visit his home because it is the only way you can determine what he wants or will buy. Notice, for example, his furniture. Is it too large for the rooms you want to show him? You won't know if you have not taken the time to find out.

It is a blessing to have just a few prospects. If you are swamped with clients, you can not visit them as often. This is especially true for a new salesman. I have noticed that the new man comes in and practically turns every inquiry into a sale. Why? Because he took the time to analyze the buyer's needs.

Keep all prospects' names. Don't assume that some are worthless and throw them away because situations change. Home financing requirements change or the buyers get extra money unexpectedly.

File your prospects' names systematically, giving those with the most money the top priority. Call them frequently. Those who are not in a hurry to buy, or who do not have the financial qualifications can wait until you are less busy.

The important thing is to know how to handle your customers. In making calls throughout the year, you can overlook the star customer. The only way to avoid this is by calling your clients frequently, by keeping in touch with them and by letting them know you are interested in their future. Frequent calls also squash the prospect's impulse to visit another real estate company.

The Prospect Priority Worksheet shown in Exhibit 7-1 is used by Rybka Realty. With it, the priority of the buyer can be established.

Exhibit 7-1

PROSPECT PRIORITY WORKSHEET

Date: _____

RANK BY ORDER OF DOWN PAYMENT; URGENCY TO MOVE!

Buyer's Name	Phone	Down Payment	Urgency to Move	Remarks
1. Carr	883-0092	30,000.	sold	call daily, show homes
2. Roberts	883-6457	25,000.	sold	call daily, show homes
3. Edwards	741-7078	20,000.	sold	call daily, show homes
4. Benner	271-6247	20,000.	tenant (lease)	call monthly
5. Tazak	886-0470	18,000.	transfer in town	call daily, work all day long
6. Malleson	886-1374	17,500.	no hurry	call on good buys, weekly
7. Moorman	341-3400	15,000.	sold	call daily, show homes
8. Barron	475-4351	12,000.	no hurry	call on good buys, weekly
9. Klein	884-4141	5,000.	no hurry	call on good buys, weekly
10. Lawler	261-6300	4,000.	sold	call daily, show homes
11. Doerr	341-3872	2,800.	must sell	try to list home first, call monthly
12. Hardy	439-1589	2,500.	lost lease	call daily, show homes daily
13. Lavin	581-2985	1,900.	renter	call monthly
14. Jackson	888-5993	1,500.	renter	call monthly
15. Palmer	248-7621	1,300.	no hurry	call monthly
16. McMillan	524-1017	500.00 GI	bills	call on nothing-to-do days
17. Manning	431-4203	450.00 GI	no hurry	call on nothing-to-do days
18. Higgins	884-0465	0 down (FHA)	if come	nothing to do, call

Even if you do not have a suitable property, you can call and say, "Mr. Lanford, this is Tom Rollins. I just want to let you know that I'll be out today looking for a home that will fit your needs and desires.

"I am really so impressed with you and your family, I am putting aside my other work and I am just going to concentrate on a home for you. So please stay home and relax. I'll do the work for you and I'll be watching the other brokers' ads as well. You don't have a thing to worry about. In a few days I'll contact you so we can have an opportunity to look at some of these homes together."

This is the way to handle your buyer so that he sticks with you and does not call other brokers. The buyer's one worry is that the real estate man won't do his job. As noted earlier, they are right 50% of the time because half of the real estate people in this world are failures.

D.B.M.–Dominant Buying Motive

People buy homes because they want them and not necessarily because they are good houses. Consider this message:

ALWAYS FAIL UPWARD

To each person who fails to buy from you, or who fails to list his home with you, convey the thought that he loses something.

He loses! He is out because he is not doing what you know he should be doing.

Always talk about him. Don't talk about yourself. You are talking about his children, his business, his promotion, or something he is doing in his life.

When the buyer purchases through somebody else, or the seller permits another company to list the property, don't write that he bought, or that she listed with somebody else. Be honest. On that card write, "I failed."

If you use this procedure, you will pause to determine how you failed. That is when you are going to start to become most successful and professional.

"I failed."

Not, "They bought from somebody else," or "They listed with another company."

"I failed."

This is very, very important!

Find out what the people want. Be in a position to convince them that what you have to offer will satisfy their wants. Then place your proposition within their reach. If you do not sell them your houses, someone else will step into your place and do it in your stead.

You must appeal to the dominant buying motives. In fact, I incorporated the DBM in our prospect sheet. Unless you have this DBM at the top of the prospect sheet, you tend to forget the dominant buying motive when you are working with a large number of prospects. I offer this example:

A hospital personnel director indicated that his wife had a bad back and that he wanted a ranch home in a certain price range. I thought that I could make the switch to a colonial or a bungalow, but after showing him such homes, he reiterated that his wife had a bad back and wanted to avoid steps. Clearly, in this case, I had incorrectly minimized his DBM.

How do you determine the DBM? Ask questions.

Some motives are the desire to stay alive . . . to be well . . . to make money . . . to feel important . . . to augment the love of family.

Other primary dominant buying motives are self-preservation, greed, pride and prestige, love of family, health and well being, the desire for advancement and the hope of getting a bargain.

Employ the emotional appeals. Behind each sale there is a desire to escape a real or imagined shortcoming. Salesmanship, therefore, is the ability to persuade prospects that they have a desire for the things that you have determined that they actually need.

Exhibit 7-2 is a Motive-Persuasion Check List that can help you in satisfying your prospects.

Remind your prospect that the home you have selected for him will answer his needs.

You might say, "When you buy this home each member of the family will have a bedroom. And, Mr. Mead living in your present home—a frame house on a small lot—does not give you accommodations as comfortable as you would like.

"Now I know that this surburban home will give you

Exhibit 7-2

MOTIVE-PERSUASION CHECK LIST

No One Buys a Home! They Buy Satisfaction of Home Ownership!

Everyone Wants Happiness; so Sell Homes by pointing out what this home will do for the buyer, emotionally. Everyone has eight emotional needs—which they demand from each purchase.

Benefits Customer Will Derive	Good Quality	Competition	Losses
1. Security—Times of stress, home is something to fall back on. Equity through systematic savings account.	1. Relative Stability of values Keeps increasing with inflation, saving actual buying power.	1. Cheaper to rent—Habits of spending.	1. Tax Benefit—rent cannot be saved—Total LOSS.
2. Comfort—ample closets, ample rooms, convenient to schools, churches, private yard.	2. Relaxation & contentment in each room.	2. Live in apt., janitor shovels snow, owner paints—pays taxes.	2. Peace of mind that you provided well for family.
3. Welfare of loved ones—children attending right schools, meeting right kids, contacts.	3. Private area for study; Excellent schools.	3. Right people and education is very important to get ahead.	3. Poor jobs; poor marriages.
4. Freedom from FEAR and DANGER Good police—fire protection.	4. Dead-end street, a safe play area for children, fenced-in yard. Brick home fire protection.	4. None.	4. Many injuries not necessary.
5. Superior Feeling—Success. Pride of Ownership; Let everyone envy you.	5. Main Street—Your name will be seen; Proper address.	5. None	5. Loss of prestige not appreciated.
6. Social Approval—accepted. Let him know who lives in neighborhood.	6. Good looking home; you're getting ahead; contact with power people.	6. None.	6. Not recognized.
7. Live longer—fresher air, healthful exercise, working in garden.	7. Keep your family together; Landscaping, family picnics.	7. Hates to work on lawn, yard.	7. Short Life.
8. True happiness—a joy to live here! Improved Romance & Love.	8. More love and affection in closely-knit family.	8. Searching for happiness.	8. Loss of love and happiness.

everything you currently lack, plus the really priceless opportunity of enjoying outdoor living."

Arouse your prospect's desire by telling him exactly what the home will do to benefit or serve him. Use visual aids, if possible. Colored photos of a home in one or more seasons of the year are especially impressive.

After you get the prospect's attention, you must maintain his interest. If you wonder if your prospect is listening, ask questions! Keep his interest by getting him to talk about himself.

Your job is to make a sale, so emphasize what the house will do for him and keep whetting his appetite.

How Benefits Become Sales Aids

Before calling on any prospect, ask yourself how the home you want to show him will benefit him in particular. Then, decide on what you are going to say to him about this house.

The following rules will help you to make sales:

1. Ask questions to arouse interest. Be sure to tell your prospect what the home or your services will do to benefit him.

2. To further arouse a prospect's desire, show him the house so he can feel it and see it, in his imagination, as the setting for his family. But be cautious in one respect; avoid exaggerated claims about the property.

3. Be sincere, always. Talk to your buyer about his problems, his profits, his home, his business, his family. Always give him an example of how the home you are offering will answer his needs. Show him that you are genuinely interested in him and his family.

After you have aroused the prospect's interest, the next job is to convince him. Be brief. Don't give more facts than your prospect needs. Determine his buying motives and direct your talk accordingly. Know at least one hundred times as much about real estate as the amount you use in your sales talk. This is the way to get people to believe in you and to respect you as an authority.

Appeal to your prospect's needs repeatedly. However, in repetition, keep changing or varying your approach to the same points. Ask questions frequently and listen to the answers. Get your prospect's views and never discuss your own.

To test his attentiveness, look him in the eye and ask, "Have I made myself clear?"

To be sure that you are giving a convincing presentation, nail down the important points as you make them. In other words, get the prospect to agree with you. Be specific throughout. State facts, not unsupported claims.

Be concrete. Make him see it, feel it, taste it, smell it. That is what I call concreteness in selling.

Be clear. Your client buys not because of what you say, but because of what he can understand. If he does not understand you, it is your fault.

Manage the interview. Don't let your prospect manage it for you.

Now perhaps you think the low-down-payment prospect isn't worth worrying about. You probably are right in assuming that you should not consume too much time with this type of prospect when there are many more-qualified customers to be served.

But let me impress you with the importance of keeping the qualifying sheets for all prospects, low-down-payment or otherwise. In short, never throw away a prospect who has given you his name and telephone number. You must realize that the person you are talking to today, no matter how far fetched it may seem, can very well be tomorrow's best qualified buyer.

To repeat, situations change. People inherit money. They work harder to save when they have given birth to the desire to buy a home. So, periodically, as time permits, call these prospects and see if they are ready and able to be converted from house wanters to house buyers.

The low-down-payment customer, if anything, is more promising than the person who seeks to buy a house contingent upon the sale of a home located in a difficult sales area. The salesman who wants to be active and successful just does not have time to be involved in such a trap. He knows it is better to ring doorbells or telephones than to invest his time in a highly improbable sales situation.

Know Your Clients

Create an aura of excitement when you want to recontact a client who has not called you recently.

Say, "Mrs. Partney, did you see our ad in yesterday's *Press?*"

Don't call and ask, "Are you still looking for a home?" That is a very poor approach. If she buys a home, you will hear about it soon enough and you won't have to ask.

But to the query, "Did you see our ad in the *Press?*" she only can answer yes or no. Either way, you will be ready.

If she answers yes, continue by saying, "I mean the home we are advertising on Pleasant Drive. The reason I am calling you is that I thought you would want to know we are getting many calls on this property. That is because there is a new, low price on this home. The family is going into an apartment and they are anxious to move. I would like to show it to you today, either at six or seven o'clock."

Now, let us assume she replies, "No, I didn't see your ad." You can remark, "Well, I am calling you because I know how busy you are and the thought struck me that you probably wouldn't have a chance to see the advertisement, but there are so many people calling! I remembered you, how nice you were, and I wanted you to have an opportunity to see this home."

At about this point, she will let you know whether they already have bought a home, or if they still are in the market.

Instill a Buying Humor

Get your client into a buying humor. When he is in the office and you are trying to sign him on a contract, he is tense and cautious. It seems to me a man can not be tense and in a buying humor simultaneously. Put the buyer in a relaxed mood. Inject a little light-hearted humor to ease the tension. Handled properly, humor can open the door to a listing or a sale.

Don't overlook the pleasantries. After you have walked into a home, look for something that can be the basis for a sincere compliment—a piece of furniture, for example.

A few years ago, I made an appointment to show a home to a young husband and wife. They had been living with her mother for 10 years and that is where I arranged to meet them. Most of the furnishings were theirs because they kept buying furniture, but never a house.

As I entered the mother's house, a knotty-pine hutch in the dining room caught my eye. I immediately walked over to it and began admiring it and opening its doors. My clients started telling me the entire history of the hutch and how long it took them to acquire it. It was their hope chest and they loved it. From that time on, I had a friendly, relaxed relationship with them. I also sold them a home.

Use Sales Conditioners

You can and should precondition a qualified prospect before showing him a listing. Here is one example of how you can sales-condition a prospect while taking him in your car to see a house:

"I feel a little sad. A client called me this afternoon and she was crying on the phone. I had shown a house to her and her husband last night. They liked it very much, but they told me they wanted to sleep on their decision. Well, the lady called to say they wanted the house, but another salesman had sold it this morning. I feel so darned bad about it. I feel it was my fault for not getting them on a contract yesterday.

"People always seem to lose when they put off a move like that. It is a shame, really!"

If your present prospect likes the home you are about to show him—if it really suits his needs and desires— you can bet he will be in a mood for immediate action.

Ease your prospect into your listing. Don't keep building up the home you are going to show him. Vary the subject. Let him talk about his hobbies. Keep him perfectly relaxed. Neutralize his mind so that when he walks into the home he can be the judge. Isn't that better than subjecting him to a big letdown?

Condition your prospect into saying "Yes!" even while you are driving him to the homes you have available. To wit: "Beautiful day, today, isn't it?"..."It was a great game, Sunday, wasn't it?" Always keep asking for that "yes" response.

You have heard that it is good manners to lead with your open paw, but refrain! Shake hands only when the buyer wants to shake your hand. Don't compel him to shake hands.

Never talk about yourself. Don't tell him how sick you are, nor about the brilliance of your youngsters. He couldn't care less. It is your job to make him feel important and in doing that, be cautious. Don't talk too much. Remember, nature gave you two ears and one mouth. Listen twice as much as you talk.

Several pages ago, I said you must know much more about the real estate business than you may ever be called upon to use. That is absolutely true, but don't get into the habit of using the real estate vernacular.

The real estate language is clear to you, but it may not be to your customer—and he never will admit it. Even relatively simple words, as they pertain to our business, may be misunderstood by the public. I am thinking of such words as listings, exclusives, rates, terms, points. Ask questions frequently to check and recheck your customer's comprehension.

Welcoming Objections

Some salesmen do not realize that quite often a prospect's objections are not objections at all. The prospect may desperately want to buy the home he is shown, but he is afraid. Therefore, he raises an objection. The good salesman realizes it is merely a plea to ease the prospect's conscience.

It should be evident that when the prospect's objections are in the form of an explanation or protest, he definitely wants to buy the home. If he had no desire for the home, you would not be called upon to make explanations.

Salesmen should not take the prospect's objections at face value; to try to argue along logical lines. Again, the prospect is voicing a plea for help.

Use these three rules to help the prospect to sell himself:

1. Show him that everybody is doing it. Point out that he owes it to himself and his family to enjoy his own home.

2. Use emotional rather than logical appeals. People buy with their emotions, not their intellect. First they want something and that makes them buy. You can paint a word picture

or two that will show that the acquisition of a home is the smart thing to do; that it will assist the prospect in maintaining his or her youth and beauty.

3. Emphasize the good things that will result from the purchase, thus overlooking any possible detracting influence. Let the prospect know that the home will provide him with an easier life. Appeal, if necessary, to his duty as a breadwinner of the family; to his need for consideration of others.

Among well-worn phrases that salesmen often employ successfully are: This home is a necessity in your modern way of life...In the long run, you'll save money...You are not spending, but actually, saving...Certainly this home is outstanding, but everyone of us is entitled to splurge once in awhile.

While the prospect may not be interested in prestige for himself, he needs what it can do for his family and for his associations with other people. Using the foregoing appeals can help allay guilt feelings that may jeopardize a sale or retard the closing.

I contend that you should talk benefits, not logic. Logical presentations invite expressions of opinion, or arguments. But when you stimulate the sales-buying emotions, you are on safer ground. Human beings seldom argue about their basic emotional needs. They all want comfort, prestige and recognition, health and safety for their children, plus long, happy lives. Who can argue with these?

I discovered the emotional appeals while just a fledgling salesman and they, more than any other factor, led to my success in selling. I jotted a list of such appeals on a pad which I kept next to me on the seat of my car. I would use these appeals, as many as possible, on each and every prospect who exhibited any interest in a property that I had shown.

My sales began to zoom because no longer was I talking about carpeting, draperies and the like. I let logic go because I felt the buyer probably would know more about double draperies, carpeting or construction than I did.

But they didn't know more about their emotions than I did!

I knew that the family, long life and social approval were

the important things to my buyers. In fact, all of us want to be accepted. So that is what I sold them. I quit selling homes and started selling the eight emotional benefits which are listed in the next section of this chapter. These eight appeals constitute the entire secret of selling.

To illustrate, let me present a brick home. You could tell your prospect about the brick and mortar, but even if you knew what you were talking about, what good would it do? He can see the brick and mortar. Instead, tell him this is a safer house, because there is less worry about fires in a brick house.

Explain that the brick home will not require periodic painting, so he will be able to live in it more comfortably. Furthermore, the elimination of paint jobs not only will save money, but also will do away with a lot of ladder climbing, and that means he probably can live a long and healthy life in the home.

Don't sell your prospects. Help them to buy! That is what people actually want. They just want to have a buddy around—that's you—to assure them that what they are doing is the right thing.

Another example:

"You won't realize how much you are going to enjoy this home until after you move in and you find that each and every one of your youngsters has his own bedroom to study in, to rest, and to get better grades.

"How wonderful it is going to be when your friends come over and see the way you are getting ahead. Once your name goes on this mailbox, next to the doctor, the lawyer and the judge. Oh, boy!

"Whoever dreamed when you were six or seven years old that you would be in this class? How wonderful it is that you are a success!"

Let me emphasize. People want improvements in their state of life, not a host of details about the nails, plaster and mechanical equipment.

Suppose you are selling Coke or Pepsi. Then push the pause that refreshes; the healthier, low-calorie count that lets you look slim and feel young. Yes, you'll find that party times are gayer when you drink a cola.

How about Cadillacs? Should you talk about the six-way seats, the upholstery, or the superior engineering? Not a chance. You need a picture of a sophisticated woman, dripping in mink and standing rather haughtily beside a long, sleek limousine. Talk about pride and prestige. "Thirty-five years old and you're getting a Cadillac already!"

Do you advertise car washes, or merchandise an idea? "Clean cars ride better." Who wants to buy dirt removal? On the other hand, nearly everyone agrees that a dirty car, somehow, feels sluggish. Right; Furthermore, there is a sense of pride and satisfaction in driving the cleanest, most sparkling car in the block.

What about mink stoles? Did you ever see one advertised as being good protection from the elements? No, but you are told it will enhance her beauty and that it will give her an emotional lift. Moreover, she can wear it with pride all year around.

So take a tip from the big merchants. Sell love and romance, pride and prestige, health and well being. These are the things people want to buy in a home. Don't be misled by what the customer tells you he thinks he wants. Satisfy him by showing him an opportunity to acquire the things you know he wants.

Appealing to the Emotions

When emotional appeals are used, a want is created. It is that want that causes people to act. This is especially true of the female of the species because a woman is motivated by her emotions to a greater degree than is a man.

Use the emotional appeals which have been stressed in our company for many years. They have proved to be very successful. Plan your work before you meet a prospect and review these emotional appeals. It takes but two minutes to read the list, yet they can help you to handle your buyer and save hours of frustration later. Your success—and it is a trait of a good salesman—will be in your ability to size up your prospect's emotions and to choose the appropriate appeal.

Men worry about being obligated by a mortgage. Women

are more influenced by the desire for prestige, comfort and labor-free orderliness. Both are interested in the welfare of their children, their spouse, their health and self-importance.

There are such other basic human needs as food, sleep and sex. In addition, people are compelled by the desire for money (and what it will 'buy) and—though they often try to hide it—the hope for eternal salvation.

You, have, then, these emotional appeals at your disposal:

1. SECURITY—In time of need, your home can be a financial bulwark. You have a systematic savings in the equity that is built into your home.

2. COMFORT—You always will enjoy having ample closet space, sufficient bedrooms for each member of the family and the convenience of nearby churches, schools, and shopping facilities.

3. WELFARE OF LOVED ONES—There is a good school system and your children can get to the modern, fully equipped school buildings safely and quickly.

4. FREEDOM FROM FEAR AND DANGER—The home is virtually hazard-free and has a fenced-in yard. There also is a safe play area in the neighborhood.

5. PRIDE OF OWNERSHIP—You will be a step ahead of your friends and relatives. Besides, there is a sense of satisfaction in being your own boss; in not having to worry about what the landlord will say.

6. SOCIAL APPROVAL—The home bespeaks your good judgment. Not only will you have a good-looking home, but you also will be in the environment you always have desired. A doctor, a judge, and a newspaper editor live within a few doors of this address.

7. PROMISE OF LONGER LIFE—There is good, unpolluted air here and a garden to work, providing healthful outdoor exercise. Your family will enjoy making this the regular gathering place for many, many years ahead.

8. HAPPINESS—All things considered, it will be a joy to live here. And isn't such happiness what you have been struggling to achieve all of these years?

Chapter Eight

Showing a Home Successfully

Before you even start to show a house to a prospective buyer, tell him, "I want to be as fair as possible with you. I want you to know I am merely here to help you. If there is something in this house, that you don't like, please tell me about it. That will help me to determine what you want. I am like a doctor. If you don't tell me what hurts, I can't help you as well."

When you plan to show the client three homes, ask after he has seen the second home, "Which of those two homes did you like best?" When he has seen all three, ask, "Now, which of the three homes did you like best?" After he has answered, ask, "Why do you like that one best?" The answers you will get will become part of your close, later in the negotiations.

If your client tells you that he likes the floor plan, the idea of three bedrooms, or that the paneled kitchen impressed him, he is expressing convictions. You should remember them and capitalize on them later.

The only way you can have this type of intimate dialogue with your customer is by convincing him that you are working with him as a friend; that there is no wall separating the real estate man and the buyer. Here is how I handle it as I begin the initial appointment to show houses to a prospect and his wife:

"Thank you for coming to us. I don't expect to find anything today we might like. Just do me one favor. As we go through these homes, tell me what you like, or don't like so I'll get an idea and can work to find something for you."

Keep them off balance by letting them think they won't be buying anything today. As we go through the homes, I frequently stop and say:

"What do you like about this home? I want to get an accurate picture of your likes and dislikes so that I won't be wasting your time or mine. I am very busy and I need a clear idea of what you need."

As they offer their opinions, the concept grows that you are not selling, you only are helping. All right, then help that couple buy a home today! That is what you should try to do, as their friend and not as a cold-hearted salesman.

In selling higher-priced homes, if the prospect is wary of getting into the price class you believe he should be interested in, tell him:

"As time goes on we all progress financially. Do not buy according to your present status, but buy according to your future status; say, five years from now. Statistics show that people make a change every five or six years. One of the reasons is that if you buy according to your present status, the standards represented by such a home will be too low for you five years from now. So, buy with faith in the government, the economy and your own ability. You will be able to live in and enjoy a higher-priced home for a longer period of time."

Forget Price

Don't let price frighten you because you are going to sell the home at market value. All homes are sold at market value. Therefore, quickly eliminate price quotations.

As a salesman, when I was asked for the price, I always told the customer, "It is not important unless you like the home. If you like a home, I promise you will get it at a fair price."

To repeat, the price is not important. If the customer is looking at homes, price should not be a factor at all until he has made a decision to buy. If you are looking for a suit and you are going through the suit rack, you don't check on the price of each suit. If you don't like orange suits, why should you be concerned with their prices.

It is the same in real estate. Price is not and should not be a factor. Never tell the buyer what the prices are unless you are trying to condition him by showing him a few homes and you want to educate him as to price.

Frequently, people come to the office looking for homes. If you are showing them pictures and they start eliminating homes because this one or that one is too high or not worth it, you are selling the wrong item. You should not be selling price, rather you should be selling a condition in life—the emotional appeals.

Without Appointment

At times it is necessary to show a home without an advance appointment with the seller. In such a case, when you have your people in your car, go to the door of the home and tell the seller:

"I have prospects in my car who can pay $10,000 down and who must move very soon. I have shown them a few homes which they didn't like. They indicated that they would like a home such as yours, or a similar type, so I would like to make an appointment for tomorrow."

Emphasize that the prospects have a good down payment. You will find that the seller will be anxious to let you show the house, saying, "Bring them in now. Why wait until tomorrow?"

Never tell the seller you just decided to show his home. Instead, excite him.

I have seen salesmen go to the door, talk to the owner and after receiving permission to show the house, turn around and yell to the prospect who is waiting in the car, "Hey, they're home. Come on in!"

Don't do that. Such a salesman might as well add, "Hurry up. I have the door open and the house is getting cold."

Be considerate of your prospect. Go back to the car. Open the car door for him. Tell him to come see the home and escort him into it. In that way he will feel that he is with you.

Consider, too, that when you are walking back to your car, the waiting prospect thinks, "He can't show me the house." Then you open the car door, smile and say, "Let's go in!" That is a surprise and important, also, because it helps to keep the buyer off balance.

Also, be sure to park across the street and at a slight angle from the house you are showing. At close range, a home always appears to be fantastically large. To achieve the best impression, it should be seen from the right perspective so that the buyer has an oblique view of the property.

Going Through the Home

Never allow the seller to remain in your presence while showing his house. He will try to help because he thinks he can do a better job of showing his home than you can. So ask him to leave. Here is one way to handle it:

Ring the bell and be admitted. "Mr. Johnson, this is Mr. Petrie. Mr. Johnson, the buyer and I would like to look through your home. Would you please sit down here while we go through?"

That takes the seller out of the picture. "Make yourself comfortable. Don't move until Mr. Petrie and I have gone through all of the property. Thank you."

To enable the seller to understand, tell him when you are alone with him, "The seller who helps show a home creates the impression that he is very anxious to sell and will take a low offer. You don't want your buyer to feel that you are that anxious to sell at a sacrifice price, do you?"

When you introduce the buyer and seller, say their names correctly and distinctly. As a preliminary aid, you can make up a clue sheet with the home address, price and names of seller and prospect. Use this sheet as a handy reference during your introductions.

Always ask the seller, "May I have the pleasure of showing your home?"

Also ask the seller if the prospect can look into the closets. Some people feel that the privacy of such areas of a home should not be violated.

In showing a two-story colonial, always show the top floor first and work your way down. Going from basement to the top will tire both you and your prospect.

Lead the parade through the home. Get the prospect behind you and go into all the rooms. You will find that a buyer will be reluctant to step into someone else's rooms unless you lead the way. Also, when going into a small room, such as a bedroom, walk immediately to the far side to allow the prospect space to move in and see the room. Open the closet doors to demonstrate the ample size of the storage areas.

Learn to anticipate. You open a closet door for your prospect because it might stick a bit and spoil the overall effect you are trying to achieve.

When you have finished inspecting the second floor and return to the living room, it is wise to sit down for awhile. I have found that in this brief pause the buyer can get a better impression of the property and have time to think.

If you know that a particular window affords a pleasant vista, walk over to the window and gaze out. You will find that the buyer will join you to see what you are looking at, saying, "My, isn't it pretty?" It is as though you had made a special point of showing him a beautiful picture.

After showing the first and second floors, send up a trial balloon by asking, "Would you like to see the basement?" This is the first of the trial closes in this house. If the prospect says, "No," ask him why. If he says one room or another is too small, that is valuable information that will help determine what other properties you will show.

Perhaps the seller will complain that you shot through the house without even seeing the basement. Be frank with him. Tell him that the buyer did not want to see more of the home because the bedrooms or the living room were too small.

Remember, you are a buddy to the buyer, so why should you make him buy a specific house? If you walk into a house and he immediately says, "Oh, no. I don't like this at all!" Say, "Fine, I have others." Leave the property promptly.

Surprisingly, you won't be in trouble with your seller, either. People—buyers and sellers alike—admire a company with professional representatives who do not force a prospect to waltz through a complete house which he does not want to see.

How about the confidence of your buyer? He has sufficient confidence in you to remark, "This living room doesn't fit." You reply intelligently, "Fine. I have others to show you now that I understand what you prefer." Who wants to waste precious hours looking at undesirable homes? Communication is important.

The real estate man who does not know what his buyer wants, who does not pause to learn, is the one who wastes time showing unwanted houses. Prospects are happy to get away from him. And they never will come back.

Looking at more expensive homes? Invite the prospect to slip off his coat and be comfortable. Hang the coat in the guest closet, walk into the living room and sit down. Let the prospect get the feel of the home before taking a leisurely tour through its rooms. Plan to spend as much time as possible in the home.

During the tour of the property, be quiet while the buyer tries to adjust to the home. After the first impression has been achieved, you can point out features which are not seen readily.

Anytime you can dramatize a home's hidden assets, do so. If it has valance lighting, don't talk about it. Instead, turn on the switch and let the lighting speak for itself.

Let your hand glide across a built-in cabinet and ask the buyer, "What would you say this wood is, cherry?"

It is effective, too, to let the buyer discover a few things himself. You ask him to turn on a light. He does and says, "That's a mercury switch." He is telling you. He tells his wife.

Don't demonstrate a home as you would a sewing machine or an automobile. Your role is more subtle.

You echo the buyer's comments. He says, "This is a spacious bedroom." Afterward, when you are talking to him in your car, you comment, "That was a spacious bedroom, wasn't it?"

Eliminate demonstration selling: "This is a light". . ."This is a door". . ."These are lined draperies." The woman who is buying a home probably is thinking to herself, "I wonder how soon I will be able to get rid of *those* draperies." Incidentally, the buyer is well aware of the fact that he is purchasing a house, not a set of draperies.

If you have been selling items, you have been doing hard selling. Start selling easier. Sell emotions and have more fun.

It is fun to stimulate buyers to react in a desired way. You must spotlight benefits they can not see. For instance, you note that there is a disposer in the sink that will get rid of garbage quickly; that the dishwasher under the counter will handle the cleaning chores while she is helping the children with their homework. You are not selling the house because it has a disposer or a dishwasher, but you are selling the happiness afforded by these work-saving conveniences.

When you delineate all of a home's features, you are defending it and the buyer is waiting to knock it down. For example, you might say, "They just spent $400 redecorating here." The buyer's reaction might be, "Yes, and in all of the wrong colors!"

The trick is to get the buyer to defend the home. Then he will buy it. Recently, a buyer and I were sitting on bar stools in the basement of a home I had been showing. I knew he liked the house and I gently criticized it, saying "Everything is perfect but the bar stools."

"What is the matter with the bar stools?" he asked.

"Your legs don't even touch the ground," I explained.

"So what the heck is it going to cost me to cut two inches off these legs?" he demanded to know. He bought the home.

Know that every time you direct the buyer's attention to a feature, he is contemplating an objection to that feature. You say, "This is a garbage disposer which will be a real convenience." He thinks, "Yeah, my kid will put his fingers in there and get them cut off." Not that he will tell you this!

I think you must be careful not to paint word pictures of every item. I feel very strongly that you must sell the emotions with which the buyer will not argue. Everyone wants to live longer. There, you might say, "With this garbage disposer, you won't have to run outside and catch cold."

At times it is difficult to determine what is salable among the features. Once, rather apologetically, I noted that a house had a coal furnace. "You can put a conversion burner in here, or toss out this furnace and put in a new gas unit," I remarked. "Not me," said the prospective buyer. "I don't want a gas furnace. My mother was lighting a central heater a few years ago when it blew up and almost killed her."

There I was, trying to sell a house by telling the prospect how to get rid of the coal furnace when, as far as he was concerned, that was one of the home's redeeming features.

In showing older homes that have electric fixtures with pull chains, call the seller in advance and ask him to turn on the lights. Then you won't have to lean and reach to put on the lights, making it obvious to your prospect that the fixtures are outdated.

Indeed, it is good to have the lights on, night or day, when showing a house. Pull open the draperies. Raise the shades. Brighten the rooms as much as possible. Lots of light helps sell a house.

Remember my coal furnace experience. Do not suggest improvements that can be made, or call attention to every detail in a house. Once you open the door and expose·the interior of the house to a prospect, keep your mouth shut! Let him lead himself normally through the home to look at all the rooms.

When you start talking about what a fine home it is, you create a barrier between you and the prospect. The more you glorify the home, the higher that barrier becomes.

Never defend objectionable features. Instead, mention attractive features that will deter objections.

Several years ago, I sold a home with a big lot and a wide picture window. I said, "Look at this beautiful view." I did not realize what an impression I had made until my buyer showed the home to her friends a couple of days later. The first thing she did was to walk into the living room, go to the picture window and say, "Look at the beautiful view." Only then did I realize that I had struck the right phrase—an appeal to the emotions.

Many salesmen assume they can accomplish more by trying to put themselves into the buyer's shoes. It is wrong because they can not accurately evaluate the buyer's intelligence, experience, sophistication, or depth of feeling. It is much wiser to give the buyer time to think; to refrain from saying anything while showing the house.

The buyer prays that you won't sell him anything; that

you will, instead, help him to buy. To keep attuned to him, be nonchalant. Say, "Let's just go looking at homes."

What is important for you to talk about? The wife walks into the house and she wants to know what she can do with her furniture. Don't tell her where she is going to place it. She will do that in her mind. If the home fits, you don't have to sell an incinerator. You don't have to sell the valance lighting, the draperies, or the carpeting. Nor will you sell the house because you do tell the customers about these extras. Later, after they tell you they want to buy the house, you can say, "It is a wise decision because in addition to the home you are getting these draperies and the wall-to-wall carpeting."

The truly professional salesman knows his responsibilities begin with his ability to help his prospect to find a house. The salesman doesn't try to sell him one. You can establish a professional relationship with your client through a display of honesty, sincerity, and cooperation.

After you have shown the right house to your prospect and he has stated his reasons for liking the house, make a special mental note of his reasons. Later, on the pretense of assembling all the facts and figures, you can use this information in closing the transaction. If a prospect asks for exact figures while you are showing a house, say, "Let's go back to the office and get all of the information."

You must keep reminding each buyer of the advantages of home ownership. For your own success, memorize the 10 "advantage" points listed in Exhibit 8-1. (See following page.)

Exhibit 8-1

USE ADVANTAGES OF HOME OWNERSHIP

The Best Social Security Number is the Number of Your Home

1. *Security.* The safe feeling that comes with ownership and knowledge that your home is a safeguard against inflation. if prices go up, so does the value of your property.
2. *Investment.* Payments on your mortgage mean you are buying something, not just paying rent. You keep owning more and more.
3. *Tax Advantage.* Your real estate taxes and the interest on your mortgage or land contract are deductible when you figure your income tax.
4. *Financial Independence.* More people have started on the road to financial independence through home ownership than any other way.
5. *Standing Credit.* You are a solid part of the community. You feel that you "belong" and home ownership gives you substantial credit rating.
6. *Environment.* Your children have a proper neighborhood in which to grow up. Your family finds itself among responsible home owners with backgrounds much like your own. You establish roots.
7. *A Cash Equity.* A well-bought home is like a savings account.
8. *Character Development.* Responsibilities of ownership develop business acumen and appreciation of financial independence and self-reliance.
9. *Peace of Mind.* Knowledge that provision has been made for your family and that the family can share in your pride of ownership.
10. *Satisfaction.* Along with the other advantages, there are many things that make life worthwhile . . . vegetables from your own garden . . . the chances for do-it-yourself projects, large or small . . . the backyard barbecue . . . the picture of your home on your Christmas cards. These heart-warming things are a very real part of owning your home.

Chapter Nine

Trial Closes Get
You Closer

Trial closes are questions or suggestions made at various times in the sales dialogue to determine if the prospect is ready to buy.

Trial closes are better than buying signals because they are under the control of the salesman. He can use them at any time during his sales talk. In fact, he should use them right from the beginning because they let him know when to ask for the order and they shorten his sales talk.

Most salesmen realize that the shorter sales talk is better. The salesman can be in the middle of a sales message, trying to get a contract signed, when relatives walk in and interrupt the proceedings. When there are interruptions or cooling-off periods, the salesman loses. Therefore, when a trial close is used to complete a deal quicker, he is on safer ground.

Keep the trial close simple and easy. You might say to your prospect, "Now when we make Mr. Jones an offer on his house, shall we ask him to leave the washer and dryer?" If he answers, "Yes," bring out the contract.

Here is another example: "Would you like to go to the savings and loan company that we do business with, or to your own bank for the financing?" If he answers in favor of one or the other, ask him if he would prefer to go Friday or Monday (a choice close). If he answers in favor of either day, start making the contract. If he says, "No, I'm not going to make an offer now," you are no worse than you were before you tried to close. So start selling again. Your attitude should be as though he had not answered your question.

The trial close forces you to do what you might otherwise be afraid to do. Most able salesmen are afraid to ask for that order. They are afraid to even approach the subject.

A sale should not be made by piling up facts and then asking for a decision. Rather, you should get a series of agreements from the prospect and then help him to make that decision. The need to take an action creeps up on the customer.

One of the best closes recommended is the "weighing close." Your customer is weighing the decision to buy or not to buy. The best thing to do is to bring that decision to a head. Say, "When we talked about buying this home earlier, you mentioned that the price was too high and that you didn't particularly like the sizes of the rooms. Are there any other reasons for not buying now?"

He will think and say, "No," or "Yes, we have another point." Then, of course, you will go back to the conviction part of your sales talk, giving the facts alone without the benefits. You will say:

"You have enough bedrooms in this house for your family. It is close to schools and transportation. It is on a 100-by-200-foot lot which you always have wanted."

In other words, you are trying to rebuild your sale. This time, without the benefits. It is just a close—and very short.

Perhaps you will consider it more important to put these points of conviction in writing for your prospect. If so, write them down and put the sheet in front of him. Then ask him, "Which weighs more, Mr. Jones? The reasons for buying, or the ideas against buying?" With such reasoning, you will get his agreement and turn it into a close.

All well and good, as far as a sales talk goes, but how ao you get him to sign that order? Get him to agree to sign the contract on a minor point. Don't ask if he is going to buy or not. That would be forcing him to make a decision. But get a "Yes" or "No" and close on a minor point.

Among questions that get the sale: "Which bank do you prefer?"..."You want to get into this new home as soon as possible, don't you?"..."Can't you picture yourself, after you move in, having all your friends over for a party in this beautiful recreation room?"

Upon getting a positive answer to any of the foregoing questions, simply turn the contract around and let him sign it.

If you are selling income property, offer the prospect some assistance. For instance, you might say, "The upstairs is empty, but as soon as you move in, I'll help you write a 'for rent' ad for the paper so that you can find tenants."

Another action inducement is the order-blank close. With this one, you ask the prospect what his initials are, or his address. If he lets you write this down in the contract, the chances are that he will let you fill in the rest. Once you begin writing the initials or address, start filling in everything else.

But if he says, "No, I won't give you my address now because I'm not ready to buy," start supporting your ideas again.

Another trial close is: "Do you wish to sign now, or have I failed to explain something to you?" You always can use this one. I think it is good because it puts the buyer on the spot and yet it does not convey too much pressure.

Let's look at some closing rules.

1. ASK FOR THE ORDER.

Everything has failed and you know you are going to lose a particular prospect. You know he has consulted other brokers and now you show him the house he really should buy. If you have tried absolutely everything else and you haven't locked him up, just point and say, "Sign this contract! This is the house for you."

If he refuses, you have not lost anything that was not beyond hope already. But don't be surprised if your customer immediately softens, needs your direct instruction and signs the contract.

2. EXPECT THE PROSPECT TO BUY FROM YOU.

No matter which home he looks at, resolve that he is going to buy from you. Salesmen are never shot for asking for an order, so don't panic. Just assume you are going to make the sale and keep on trying. This is a part of your business and you must do it and keep at it for the rest of your life.

3. KEEP A STRONG POINT IN RESERVE.

Have a strong point about your house in reserve. Then in the event that your prospect balks at the point of buying, you can advance this strong point to close the transaction.

One such stonng point might be the draperies (providing you have not committed the error of trying to list all of the house's good points too early). You can tell the prospect who is not quite convinced, "Don't forget, the draperies are included."

Try to hold back a feature that you know the buyer will want sufficiently to turn the tide.

4. BEWARE OF THE ASSUMPTIVE "NO!"

Each time a salesman and a prospect get together, a sale is made. Either the salesman sells the prospect, or vice versa. Therefore, at a certain point in the sale, you can assume a sale is made and act accordingly. This is an assumptive close.

But only a few salesmen realize that the same psychology can be used by the prospect on the salesman. Thus, salesmen often become victims of the assumptive "No."

Review some of your own lost sales. Did the prospect say, "No," or did you merely assume that that was what he meant? Prospects dread to tell you, "I am not going to buy from you." They will say, instead, "Well, I'll think it over," or "I can't afford it." Often, when a salesman hears such remarks, he assumes the prospect is not going to buy, so he quits. His own favorite tool has been used against him.

But when the average salesman who thinks he has heard "No" leaves, that is precisely when the star salesman starts selling. Anybody who has specialized in getting listings knows that sellers "No" you to death, but they are also the same people who stand there and keep on talking. Frequently you can turn the conversation into a positive channel by saying, more as a suggestion than a command, "Please sign your name as you usually do," or, "You should sign first, Mr. Jones."

Never leave a prospect until he has said "No" at least seven times.

5. USE AN HONEST HOOK.

An honest hook also is called a hurry-upper. To explain, you want to give reasons why the prospect should buy now. Here is the hook: "We'd better hurry to see this home right now. Another salesman is scheduled to show it later." In other words, let's beat the crowd and get that house before somebody else does

6. SAVE A FINAL QUESTION.

Save one good question until the end. Example: "Why put off this offer overnight? Your wife loves this home. You want to make her happy, don't you?" That "make wife happy" suggestion is an emotional appeal, of course, that can be used effectively in many sales situations.

7. ACT AS THOUGH SIGNING IS ONLY A ROUTINE MATTER.

(Even when your heart is in your mouth!)

8. AVOID PROCRASTINATIONS.

Never agree to call back on a prospect until you have tried every known way of closing on the spot and failed. Each time a prospect succeeds in delaying you, or in putting you off, you become less effective in your next attempt to make that sale. (Better jot that down and put a red circle around it.)

Realize, too, that before you can recontact your prospect, a competitor can get to him and sell him a different property.

9. USE AN EXAMPLE AS A FINAL PUSH.

And here is an example of that example at work: "Let me tell you about a party in the same position you are in."

Let the prospect know that he is not alone. Let him know

that others have been just as nervous as he is about signing a
contract. You might use yourself as an example—"You should
have seen how hesitant I was before I bought my first house"—
especially if you have established a good rapport with your
customer.

10. GET THE CONTRACT IN VIEW EARLY.

Even though you are just taking the prospect to look at a
house, have a contract in sight in your car. You want the
prospect to see it. You want him to be familiar with it. Then,
when you are ready to use it, you won't have to pull it out like
a concealed weapon and scare the daylights out of him.

11. MAKE REFUSALS DIFFICULT.

The point is, it should be harder for your prospect to refuse
than to go ahead and buy.

Fill out the contract. The prospect must either stop you,
or put himself in a postition where he has a moral obligation to
sign it.

Truly, it is not an important-looking document. When you
start filling it, he figures that he better stop you before you can
finish the form. If he does not stop you, you are set. All that
you need is his signature, and at this point, you can get the signature almost every time if you proceed in a calm manner. Just
turn the contract around and say, "Sign it." It works!

Chapter Ten

Overcoming the
Prospect's Objections

There is one word that you should stop using and that is "offer."

Do not plant the thought in the prospect's mind that he can buy this house for a lower price than you have quoted. So forget the word "offer." Eliminate it from your vocabulary.

Weighing the Reasons

In the trial close you present the reasons why the prospect should buy. In using the weighing close, you get the prospect to expose himself.

You say, in effect, "Here are the reasons why it is smart to buy this property. And on the other hand, here are the ideas why you don't want to buy. Don't you agree the reasons for buying are better than the ideas against buying?"

To the proposal that the buyers get a blanket mortgage, they frequently will ask, "Is that good?" You must be careful at all times that you do not tell people to do something. You never tell them to buy. You never tell them to do anything. You give them ideas and let them make the decisions.

For instance, in answering that question about the blanket mortgage, you might say, "Other people who have bought

123

homes from us tell us that the convenience loan, or blanket mortgage, is extremely good. They are happy they used it."

If the prospect remarks, "I heard about a fellow who lost a lot of money on a blanket mortgage," you can answer the objection in this way:

"The only situation in which you can get hurt is if you try to sell your house for more than its market value. You are going to price your present house fairly, aren't you?"

He will say, "Oh, sure. We don't want more than a fair price."

Keep Asking Questions

Ask the prospect more questions. You still have to find the buying signal.

Here is a good question often used successfully by the Rybka salesmen in persuading a buyer to assume a blanket mortgage:

"Don't you think your home will sell? Is there something wrong with it?"

Immediately, the buyer defends his property. "Of course it will sell!" he exclaims.

"Then, if you are sure your property will sell, you have no reason not to take this convenience loan, this blanket mortgage. Right?"

Make him defend his property and he will go ahead with the purchase and blanket mortgage.

Now let's say you have a buyer who is interested in a home. You are trying to lock him up, but he is telling you to go; that he wants to sleep on it. God is going to help him overnight and he will be back with the archangels to make a deal with you.

Right?

Wrong!

There is no second shot with such a person. You must look upon each buyer as a last shot. If he walks out, you are through with him. Start looking for another buyer.

Get the procrastinator to expose one reason for delay. The balance of the reasons, then, are of no value. Perhaps his one principal reason is, "I don't want to go into a blanket mort-gage." Then reiterate his chief reason.

Salesman: "The chief reason, you say, is you don't want the blanket mortgage. Is that right?"
Buyer: "Right."
Salesman: "Otherwise you would buy this home if it wasn't for a blanket mortgage. Correct?"
Buyer: "That is about it."
Salesman: "Sir, what is wrong with your house? You don't think it is going to sell, do you?"

Now he has to defend his principal exposed reason.

You, as the salesman, also will have given that buyer a choice of three homes. Now which one of these homes does he like? Let him pick the property so that you won't be selling the wrong one, nor will you be pushing one that you think he ought to like. Secure in the knowledge of his choice, you will be content to sell him the house you personally thought was a "dog."

"How Have I Failed You?"

When your prospect prepares to leave, stating that he will decide overnight, ask:

"What have I failed to explain because you are going to worry about it all night. This is very bad. You shouldn't be thinking and thrashing the ideas out at home. I have all the information for you, here.

"How have I failed? Somewhere I did not explain some item. Something is bothering you. You could still go home. All I want to do is to settle this for you, now, so you don't have to go home and worry about it."

This is probing.

Ask him seven times.

If he says, "No, I'm still going home. . .I'm going home. . .I'm going home. . ." you can let him go home, but keep asking him:

"Where have I failed? Why should you worry about it? Let me help you make a decision, now.

"Others have told us that they were glad that we did this for them. These are the things we want to do for you."

Eliminate Signature Worry

When they are signing the contract, talk about something besides real estate.

As soon as the form is prepared for signing, you always should say to the sellers or to the buyers, "The husband always signs first," or, "Mr. Smith, you sign first and your wife signs second. You must sign here."

Certainly you recognize that it is important to eliminate any area of fear for your customer when you want him to sign the contract. So do this:

You have completely filled the purchase agreement form and you are about ready to ask for the buyers' signatures. You should sign the form first as the witness. This eliminates their fear about doing something which is overwhelmingly legal.

Make out the entire agreement. You sign first and let them sign next to you. For the buyers, it removes the pressure of being the first to sign this dreadful document.

Throughout your selling effort, you let your customer talk. If he attacks the property, let him talk. Don't defend the property! Let him tell you everything that is wrong with it; why he doesn't want to buy it; everything or anything else. Let him keep talking and let it get out of his system.

Now, while he is signing the contract, take the pressure off him so that he won't be concerned with the magnitude of his actions. Sidetrack his worries with an observation such as, "What do you think of the Browns?" Or, "They say this is the year we can expect the Yankees to make a comeback. They were first to go into spring training. Isn't that something?"

As soon as the customers have signed, congratulate them upon having done the right thing.

Say, "You won't realize what a wonderful decision you made tonight until six months from now when you sit back and fully appreciate what a great thing you did. Congratulations!"

Shake their hands. Then beat it.

In one of my closings, the fellow was so tense and so

nervous, I could almost see him tearing off his fingernails. I gave him the photo-listing of the home and asked, "Will you help me? I'll show you how this is made out. See if you can figure out what the lot size is. . .What was that address again? . . ."

He and his wife were looking at the listing and reading the listing information. I was writing as fast as they were telling me what was on the sheet. "Carpeting?" I was writing while they were checking and telling me.

May I say that when the people are signing the contract, the pressure is on you, too. It feels good to say something to the buyer because you might be scared, but talk about something other than real estate.

When I was a novice, the greatest pressure I felt was when I had floor duty and people walked into the office. I would almost pass out. I could answer phones with confidence, but when a stranger came in, I trembled. It was sheer worry that I would lose an obviously good prospect.

In the event that your prospect is walking out, or let's assume that he came back and you must lock him up, tell him immediately that you are there to help him. "I am not trying to sell you. I am here to help you."

Get that message across and you will be on his side. It is not combat between the seller, the buyer, a salesman or a closer. The customer simply is not sure whose side you are on. So tell him, "I am here to help you. I am not here to tell you to sign. I don't care." Very important.

When a man complains about the price, always ask him to substantiate why the price is high. Frequently, a real estate salesman will immediately think that such a man is saying, in effect, that he doesn't want to buy the property. The remark, "Your price is too high," must be rephrased and considered as a question, "Tell me, why is it so high?"

That is how you have to understand a high-price remark. It is a problem, of course, on higher-priced homes or income properties.

Buyer: "Your price is too high."
Salesman: "Do you like the home?"
Buyer: "Yes, but it is too much." (Actually, he is saying,

"Why are you asking so much for this property?" Counter his remark by using the reproduction appraisal; especially if you know that the reproduction figure is greater than the sale price. Perhaps in listing the home you appraised it for $18,900 and later it was reduced to $17,000.)

Salesman: "Well, look, I want to show you our confidential file. Don't tell anybody I showed you this. I could get in trouble with the manager. See what we appraised this home at?"

You must convince him that the value of the property far outweighs the price.

If the customer is ready to buy, but isn't signing, you must inquire further:

Salesman: "Something is holding you back. Tell me your ideas for not making a decision. Maybe I can help you."

Buyer: "Well, I want to buy the house, but the price is too high."

Salesman: "Why?"

Buyer: "I don't want to buy it because it is too far from transportation."

Salesman: "Why?"

Buyer: "Really, I don't want to buy it because. . . ."

Salesman: "Why?"

Soon you will find if you provide enough "why's" to expose his objections, he will buy.

Two Main Objections

One customary objection is, "The price is too high." The other principal objection is, "I'll think about it."

As explained earlier, when the customer says he is going to think about a property, he actually has an objection and you can't let him go. Stay with him until you learn why he wants to go home to think about it, or why he wants to call you back. Keep searching and probing until you know the real objection.

Another way to answer objections is to admit them.

Buyer: "Boy, this house really is run down."

Salesman: "Yes, you are right. It is run down."

He figures this is his big objection. This is the big thing

that is going to get him out of buying. He is going to say, "This house really is run down." You say, "Yes, you're right." That is it. Pass it by as though he never even said it.

Remember, the buyer wants to buy. Let him buy! Don't sell him. He doesn't want to be sold. He doesn't even want to be sold on a close. He wants you to let him make the decision. So you want to create the impression that he is buying: you are not selling him. Make the customer feel important.

The close is partially locked up because of the lister's previous contacts with the seller. When the offer comes in, the seller is primed and ready for that offer.

On the other hand, if your office has not maintained contact with the seller for two or three months and you go to him with an offer, you will have to face, first, a barrage of anger. So part of the closing game is to keep in contact with the seller.

Sears Roebuck has all of the objections to the company or its products canned; that is, written down. Any Sears employee can be transferred to another department and will be prepared to handle objections in the new department. For instance, if a man is transferred to the water tank department, he will have a manual there which will list all of the common objections to the store's line of water tanks. With this advance information, he will be equipped to answer the objections as they are raised.

You can defend price if you know exactly what the house has to offer and what the sales tag includes. It is better, however, to know the number of houses that have been sold in a recent period for that same price. Use this information in reverse when you are closing; show the seller what his house is bringing in relation to the market. Also, show the information to the buyer so that he will know what similar houses cost. This is comparison selling and it helps to justify the price.

When you are showing a home, you should have copies of recent utility bills for that property. Naturally, the buyer of a $90,000 home with two or three furnaces isn't going to tell you he is worried about the size of the gas bills. And yet, he very well could be concerned for many people are generous with dollars, but tight with pennies.

If the prospect says to you, "The fuel bills must be awfully high," you'd better know what they really are, or you are going to be stuck. If you failed to get all of the facts in advance, you will have to go back to your office, call the sellers and get the fuel bill figures.

In the weighing close, the psychological moment is not readily noticeable, so state:

"Mr. and Mrs. Adams, in a little while you are going to make a decision. First, let us enumerate the ideas which would offer opposition to buying the property and the reasons that favor such a purchase."

Now, anything he can advance which is against buying is an "idea." Everything you have presented which supports the purchase is a good "reason." So overcome any objections. What he is saying is only an idea.

Here is a technique which has been very successful for me. After the buyers have signed the contract and I have handed them their copy, I say to them, "Wish me luck and keep your fingers crossed. Better yet, when you get home, say a prayer for me because I am going to need it."

Thus, with this "calmer," the buyers will not be thinking about backing out of the deal. They will be more anxious about the sellers' acceptance. They will be hoping and praying that you will be able to close the sale with those sellers.

Sometimes when I return with the contract signed by the seller, I give them a fight story in reverse and the buyer's wife will say she was praying that I would get the home for her.

You wouldn't want to run back to the buyers and say, "Well, here it is. You've got it!" They might think they paid too much. This, I submit, is one reason why the selling man should be at all closes. Otherwise, how would he know what happened and what counter measures should be made?

Buyers and sellers think they are trying to conquer each other. You only are their instrument of selling or getting a home. Tell them about the hard-fought battle so they will know what a great victory they won.

Chapter Eleven

How to Cope with Buyer Fears

Watch the salesman who talks himself out of a sale and resolve not to make the same mistake. Such a man keeps talking and does not heed the buying signals. His chatter carries him and his prospect beyond the highest point of enthusiasm and once that has happened, the buyer begins to oppose the purchase.

The good salesman, however, will ask tactfully, "How soon would you like to have possession?" . . . "Would you like the carpeting to stay?"

If you are certain that a prospective purchaser likes a home and yet he refuses to sign, ask why. Remember to keep probing until you expose his objections.

It is well to realize that the average buyer greets that dotted line on the contract with a great deal of trepidation. This is especially true of the young, first-time home buyers. With first-time buyers, I like to keep the contract in sight and then proceed in this way:

Salesman: "Did you ever buy a home before?"
Buyer: "No."
Salesman: "Well, sooner or later you are going to buy a home so I will demonstrate to you how a purchase agreement

works. Let's use the home you like fairly well as an example. Let me read this to you."

Then you take the form and start reading the purchase agreement—and you start filling in the blanks. Let the buyer cooperate with you.

Salesman: "Single frame colonial with two-car garage. Price?"

Buyer: "Oh, if we were to buy, the highest we would go would be $18,500."

Salesman: "$18,500. That is $8000 down. If you did want the home, how would you want the title? In your wife's name, your name, or joint tenancy title?"

Buyer: "What is that?"

Salesman: "A joint tenancy title is one in which you and your wife have both your names on the deed."

Big problems become little problems. The salesman knows the buyer will forget the major problem because the average person only thinks of one thing at a time.

Salesman: (With showmanship, now) "What is your full name?"

Buyer: "James Robert Davis and Alda Louise Davis."

Salesman: "Do you want the seller to leave the carpeting, if you buy?"

Buyer: "No."

Salesman: "How soon would you want to move in?"

All of these little obstacles are explored and in so doing, the major problem of buying a home is minimized.

Salesman: "All right, we are finished. Now you understand what a purchase agreement is all about. Are there any questions?"

Buyer: "Can't think of any."

Salesman: "Well, initial this and I'll go to work and see if I can get it for you."

To that remark, the buyer might exclaim, "Hey, what's this? C'mon, I'm not buying!" That is a possible outcome, but sometimes the technique outlined here is successful. Even more often, you will find that many buyers must be pushed into the homes they really want. Fear makes them reluctant to complete the transaction.

You will learn that fear is a common problem among prospects, no matter who they are, nor what price range they are buying in. Your role in real estate is service; to relieve the buyer of the ugliness of fear.

Medical journals state that fear kills thousands of persons each year. Be assured that fear also has killed many a real estate deal. To help people, you must be able to provide truthful, positive and satisfactory explanations for each and every negative fear that would divert your buyer. If you are not qualified to do that, someone else will do it in your stead.

Your job is to expose hidden fears and objections so that there will be true understanding. Frequently the buyer will conceal his real fear behind a little white lie.

Popular Fears*

The first such fear is the supposition that it might be cheaper to rent than to buy. Here is how our salesman handled this problem. He made an appointment to see some prospects after he had shown them a home. They did not want to buy the home because they thought possibly it would be cheaper to stay in rent.

The salesman drew a large square and showed the prospects that this large square, representing the living area in the home they had seen, would cost them $85 a month. Then he drew a smaller square which represented the amount of living area they had in the house they were renting for $100 a month. The result: it was costing them $15 more a month to have the use of smaller space. Also, if they bought, the interest and taxes would be deductible and the remaining principal would be money saved. Rent money, once paid, could never be redeemed. With this explanation by the salesman, the buyers were convinced.

Now here is another buyer who says, "I'm only paying $60 a month for rent and the payments on the house you are

*This Section is adapted from: *Brass Tacks of Real Estate Selling,* by Ray Smith, 310 Arballo Drive, San Francisco. Copyright 1955 by Ray Smith.

offering would be $125. It is cheaper for me to stay where I am."

What can you say to that buyer? Obviously, you should point out that the $65 difference is buying him a much larger home and more family happiness, but let the dollar figures work for you, too. Show him that the amount of money going into principal is merely going from one of his pockets into another. There also are the benefits of income tax deductions for interest and real estate tax.

It should not take too long to prove that the real difference between monthly payments and rent is about $10 rather than the $65. Then get enthusiastic about how much more he is getting for that little $10 bill.

Let us assume that your buyer is taking a $10,000 mortgage at 6%. That would mean $600 per year in interest, or an average of $50 per month. Such interest is the only part of the payment which is equivalent to rent and it is the rental fee for the use of money. Furthermore, the $600 in interest is tax deductible and that means a savings of 20%, or $120. Therefore, technically, he only is paying $40 a month rent on the house that you are suggesting he buy.

A second fear is that prices will come down; that it might be better to wait. Such a fear can be answered by explaining to the prospect that what they will buy always is in the same price market as what they sell. In other words, if a man paid $20,000 for a house five years ago and found that in the current market it was worth only $14,000, he would not actually be losing money. Why? Because if he did indeed sell the house for $14,000, he could use the money to go back into the same market and buy another house that also would be priced proportionately lower than its value five years earlier.

A third common fear is that if the national economy drops and a man is forced to take a cut in pay, he might not be able to keep up with his payments. The answer, of course, is that the government would step in, as it did in the last depression, and payments on loans would be adjusted at a fair ratio to the national income.

Fear No. 4: If a man gets sick or loses his job, he will lose his home.

Answer: If it is an extended illness, it is possible that he could double up with relatives and rent his house for a figure higher than his monthly payments. Concerning the fear of death, it should be noted that comparatively cheap mortgage insurance is available which guarantees full payment of the mortgage balance in the event of the death of the wage earner.

Fear No. 5: A home owner will lose much money if he is transferred to another locality. The assumption here is that the amount of the commission and the high initial interest payments would be money lost in the short run.

To answer Fear No. 5, assume that the owner of a $40,000 house is transferred after two years. He paid a $2400 commission, bringing the house down to $37,600. Now let's say he can sell the house for at least $35,000—a cut of $5000. However, if the owner had rented a house of comparable size, it would have cost him $500 a month, or a total of $12,000 in two years. Therefore, even though his investment plan is upset, the owner is better off with his brief title to the property than he would have been as a tenant.

Fear No. 6: Beware of hasty decisions; it is better to get spiritual guidance by sleeping on it. This is the fear most often expressed, but it is an excuse for a deeper fear that can be revealed with a better selling job.

Bring Buyers Into the Office

It frequently happens that after the prospects have been shown a few homes and it is apparent that they like one of the choices, they are reluctant to make any commitment.

How do you get such a prospect to re-enter your office? Say, "Let's go inside for a minute. I don't have all the information on this particular home; the taxes, lot size and so forth."

The prospect says to himself: "I am not buying. He is just going to give me a little more information that he has in the office. But it is not going to change anything."

With the prospect back at your desk, begin to probe. You learn that he thinks the price is too high, so . . .

Salesman: "How high? If you were to make an offer, would you buy it at your price?"

Prospect: "Yes, I would."

Salesman: "Let's try and get it for you at your price. What is your price?"

Prospect: "Well, you said it is a $40,000 house. Could be, but I think it is only worth $35,000."

Salesman: "How many years do you expect to live in this home?"

Prospect: "Oh, heck, I don't know."

Salesman: "Couldn't we say that it is safe to expect that you will live in that home for 10 years? If you live in it for 10 years, that means that it is too high by $500 a year. If you live in the home only 10 months a year, it is too high by $50 a month. How many days in the month will you live in the home? If it is 30 days, then the home is too high by $1.70 a day. Don't you think that this home, fitting all of the needs of your family, is worth $1.70 more per day than your idea on price indicates? You could stop shopping and start enjoying this home immediately."

Never refuse to write the prospect's final offer, no matter how low or ridiculous it may seem. It is a start—something down on paper—and as the prospect is going home, you want him to feel that he bought a house.

Recall that when he was re-entering your office, he had said, "I am not buying. I just want some more information." That is the real joy of real estate. It is a friendly game in which you match the buyer with a home and everybody is happy ever after.

Let us assume, now, that you still are having some difficulty in getting the prospect to commit himself. You remark, "Sooner or later, you are going to buy a particular property. Let me bring you up to date on the financing, today.

"This specific property is $25,000. You are going to use what, ten down? Your payments will be X dollars. How does that sound to you? Of course you could move in within 30 days."

When a buyer asks, "Does the carpeting and draperies stay?" ask him in return: "Do you want the carpeting and draperies to stay?" If the reply is in the affirmative, he has bought a home!

You continue to press for the close by commenting, "Let's put all of this down so that you can have a copy of it." You then fill out the contract. When you are finished, just turn it around and say to your customer, "Initial it here, please."

But now come more objections, including the familiar refrain, "We want to sleep on it. If the house is right and God is willing, it will be here tomorrow for us to buy."

"Isn't it possible," you inquire, "that at this given moment, somebody is praying to God that he can find a good house and that God will decide that this house is the one for him? God could be watching you and saying, 'You are not helping yourself. I'll help the other man who also is asking for my assistance.' Instead of asking God to keep the house on the market for you, you should be saying, 'God, I am buying this home. Bless me so it will be a good deal.'

"Just imagine if God had a switchboard. A call comes in. It is a farmer saying, 'I need rain for my corn. It has been too dry.' Next, another call comes in. It is a little boy saying, 'God, we are going on a picnic. Please make it a warm, sunny day.' God has a problem. A farmer who needs rain. A boy who wants to go on a picnic.

"Isn't it a lot more logical to just buy the home and ask God for his continued blessings?"

The point is, you are not attacking God, but you know the prospect is hiding behind God. And you have to remove that obstacle to get at the true objection.

Now here is another problem.

Your prospect tells you: "I like the home and I do want to buy it, but this is the year for a new wage contract in our plant and now it looks as though we will be out on strike, maybe three or four months. If that happens, I wouldn't be able to keep up with the payments on the house, so I think that I had better wait."

How do you overcome this problem? He has to live some place, of course, but he already had told you that his rent is $50 per month and the payments on the house that you have shown him would be $125. That could be a tough amount to meet for the man who is on strike. And yet you are not defeated. You can answer in this way:

"I am sure that you realize that in any prolonged difficulty, you would be able to rent out your house.

"That not only would help you to keep it, but with any luck at all, there would be a little extra realized from the rent which would help to relieve a desperate situation.

"Then, too, you are in the steel mill and the banks are cognizant of the fact that many of their customers are affected by industrial strikes. They don't really want to foreclose. That means they would allow you and the others who are in the same situation to pay the interest on the mortgage and forget about the principal until you get back to work. You will never be in default as long as you pay your interest. You can even have an adjustment made to set aside your taxes temporarily."

Consider the strike issue as another excuse offered by the buyer. He realizes that he is on the verge of buying a home and he is afraid. You must be able to allay these fears.

The buyer says he might be laid off. Tell him that he will get unemployment benefits. Then he will get $50 to $55, so he will be able to meet his interest payments. He won't be able to eat steaks, but he will be able to make his interest payments and at the same time eat a lot of hamburgers.

At this point, the wife usually turns to her husband and asks, "What is steak?"

The fear of losing a job is seldom mentioned by a buyer who is considering a higher-priced house. But it is a very real fear among the no-down-payment buyers.

Here's a true story: I had a customer call me. The man and his wife were in the bank when he learned that he was being laid off. He panicked. He told me that he worked for a bakery. I asked him how long he had worked there. About four years, he replied. I asked for his boss' name and immediately called him.

"How long will Mr. Hughes be out of work?" I inquired.

"It is seasonal; happens every Christmas," he answered. "Bill Hughes won't be out of work for more than two weeks."

I recalled Mr. Hughes and told him what I had learned from his boss. Said he, "Oh, my God. I am so happy. I figured that I would be out for three or four months." Reassured, he went ahead and bought the home.

Let that be a tip. Don't be afraid to call the buyer's personnel department to eliminate such fears.

Frequently we have occasion to call a local steel mill. Invariably, the report is, "Oh, we are going to call him back in 10 days. It is just a temporary shutdown to make repairs in his division." That type of information has helped us to salvage many a deal.

In handling the fear of layoff, the ideal circumstance is that in which the prospect's monthly payments will be the same as his present rent. Then we say, "If you are going to be laid off, won't you have to pay any rent? Oh, you will? What, then, is the difference if you are paying rent, or your house payment? They are both the same amount."

Chapter Twelve

How to Make the Most Sense with Dollars

You will be well on your way to success in a transaction when you know how to overcome interest rate objections. For example, your client is excited about a house. The mortgage will be $20,000 and the amount of interest is 8%.

Buyer: "I like the house, but I've just been figuring it out. If I pay 8%, in 30 years I'll be paying at least $40,000 on this house. On that basis I can't buy it. Find me something cheaper."

Salesman: "Would you take the home if I could get you a 2% loan?"

Buyer: "Are you kidding?"

Salesman: "No. I am serious. If I can get you a 2% loan on $20,000, would you take the home?"

Buyer: "Sure."

Salesman: "That is what I have for you. A 2% loan."

Buyer: "How do you figure?"

Salesman: "What would be the ideal way for you to buy a home?"

Buyer: "If I had the dough in the bank, I could buy it for cash. No mortgage."

Salesman: "But you would be losing 6% on your savings account."

Buyer: "That's true."

Salesman: "Even if you pay the cash for a home, you still are paying interest. Everybody pays interest on a home. If you have it paid off, you are losing the amount of interest you would be getting on savings at the bank—6%. Actually, you don't have the $20,000, but you can get it for 8%—only 2% more than if you were using your own money."

Additional details shown in Exhibit 12-1 prove the point. For prudence sake, it is better to borrow.

Exhibit 12-1

IT'S BETTER TO BORROW

$10,000—DEPOSITED OR BORROWED

Term	Savings Deposit @ 6%	Mortgage @ 8%	Difference
5 Years	$13,842.33	$12,166.20	$ 1,676.13
10 Years	18,602.93	14,559.60	4,043.33
15 Years	25,000.78	17,202.60	7,798.18
20 Years	33,598.95	20,076.00	13,522.95
25 Years	45,154.17	23,157.00	21,997.17

An Answer to the Cash Buyer—Many home buyers think it would be better to pay cash, rather than to borrow and pay mortgage interest money. The table above shows that it is actually cheaper to get a real estate loan than to take the money out of a personal savings account. The buyer who borrows $10,000 for 25 years at 8% pays $13,157.00 in mortgage interest. If he elected to withdraw the $10,000 from his savings account, to pay cash, he would save the mortgage interest, but he would lose the interest on his savings, totaling $35,154.17 in 25 years. The difference, therefore, means the cash transaction would cost him an additional $21,997.17.

Now here is another buyer who doesn't like the interest rate.

Buyer: "8%, points and all that stuff! For the rest of my life I'll be behind the proverbial eight-ball at this rate."

How do you overcome the fact that he will be strapped with an admittedly high interest rate? Consider the following comment:

Salesman: "Do you really think that? Look, you are only putting 10% down on this fine property, but after you have accumulated more equity in the house you can speak to the lender and get the rate reduced. You realize that, don't you?

"You don't even have to refinance it. All you have to do is to go back and say, 'Now I have 20% equity. The 20% buyer is getting X rate. I'd like my rate to be adjusted downward. If you can't do it, I'll have to refinance it somewhere else.' The bank will cut the rate automatically. It doesn't want to lose a good customer. The mortgage does not change. It is just a matter of bookkeeping—a change in the monthly payments, so there is no additional cost.

"I had a customer with 10% down who wanted a 7¾% rate. We were able to get him a 8% loan with the understanding that when his equity picture improved, he would be able to get a lower rate. And that is what he did."

Frequently, people are afraid to give you a cash deposit and they also are afraid to sign the note. To ward off these worries, I put on the top of every note and into every contract this statement: "Deposit to be returned if deal does not go through."

Let the buyer know that if a satisfactory arrangement is not found that he will not lose anything. It is important that you know how to deal with this very deep, very real buying fear. As you persist in the closing, tell the buyer you need a deposit—not cash.

"Do you have a thousand dollars? No, well I will tell you what I'll do in your case. We will make a note and I will put on top, here, if this doesn't work out, it doesn't cost you anything."

That should be part of every sales talk because it reassures your customer.—"It costs you nothing if you don't get this property at your terms."

But remember, that with an FHA loan, there is a $45

charge—the cost of the appraisal and credit report—if the deal does not go through."

The buyer will be raising plenty of objections which, again, are requests for help. If you have the answers and give him more information, it eliminates the pressure of selling.

Assume, now, that you have a buyer who wants a specific feature or improvement in the property. Perhaps he wants storm windows, or he wants the house to be painted, or he wants something else done that he thinks is needed. How would you handle this? Would you put the demand into the contract? I suggest that you recommend a financial adjustment and let the buyer take care of his own improvements. It may not be the right time, for instance, to paint the house.

"You want the storm windows and this will cost $40? All right, let's get the price reduced by that amount. No, let's cut it down $50."

Or . . .

"The home is $19,500. Now you want it painted? As you know, this isn't the best time of the year to get a house painted. How much would a paint job cost? $500? $600? Let's get the price of the home cut by that amount. In fact, let's go in for $18,900 and that will give you a little extra in case you need it."

If the buyer says the home needs redecorating, tell him that is a good reason he should consider buying it; that he can redecorate it to suit his own taste.

Above all, you do not want a situation that will complicate the closing with the seller. Why should he paint the house? That is one reason he is selling it. So for you, the salesman, it is easier to adjust the price $600 for that paint job. The new owner probably will do it himself for about $100, anyway.

Handling An Offer By Telephone

Three days after he has been shown a home, a prospective buyer calls the office. Does this sound familiar?

Buyer: "Will they take $16,000?"

Salesman: "Well, that's $2000 off. Will you give me $17,000? I'll fight for you."

Buyer: "Nope. Can't do it."
Salesman: "How about $16,500?"
Buyer: "No. $16,000."
Salesman: "I'll be right down."

After the salesman gets to the prospect's house, the latter says, "I'll go $16,000, but try $15,500."

That used to happen to me. I would have a low-ball offer and not a chance to close the deal until I watched a real pro in action. He had shown a home for $17,990. Three days later, a call came in. Notice how he handled it:

Buyer: "Will they take $16,000?"
Salesman: "I'll tell you sir, the home was shown today. I'm going to check the board and see if it is still available." (Putting the call on hold, he leaned back in his chair and lit a cigarette.)

Meanwhile, I said to him, "That home still is available." He replied, "I know. Just keep still a minute."

Picking up the receiver again, he heard the prospect's wife asking in the background, "Stan, what did he say?" "He is checking to see if it is sold." "Stan, if that home is sold, I'll leave you."

Ending the long pause, my friend the pro said:

"I've got good news for you. The home *is* available."

Stan, the buyer, exclaimed: "Listen, stay there! We will be right down."

Within eight minutes the buyer was in the office, wearing a T-shirt, slacks and dirty loafers. His wife was about 50 feet ahead of him. Their offer was $17,500.

Now that was a typical low-offer man trying to get a $17,900 house for $17,500 after originally suggesting a $16,000 offer. Why? Because the pro had changed him emotionally.

I quickly learned that I had been doing two things wrong. First, I tried to do business on the telephone, which is wrong! Second, by agreeing to the prospect's low price, I made him think the home probably was only worth $16,000.

The Right Moment

The psychological buying moment can range from a few

seconds to a much longer period. Often, as much as a month. This means, therefore, that if you miss the psychological buying moment, you don't necessarily lose the sale. Rather, look for buying signals as you continue to use trial closes in your sales talk.

You will find the buying signals in what the prospect does and in what he says. For example, when he relaxes, opens his hands, leans forward, or assumes a more pleasant expression. He shows his agreement by nodding his head, by uncrossing his legs, or in picking up the purchase agreement (which is a decidedly good buying signal).

Perhaps he will have an unusual sparkle in his eye, or he will do something which indicates purchase action. He might say, "Well, we can put the piano here and our television set over there."

That is the time to stop immediately and ask him to initial the purchase agreement.

When the husband says to his wife, "Mama, what do you think?" You know one of them is sold. Then it is up to you. Ask for the order because one of them is on your side already.

Among other remarks that are good buying signals are: "Suppose I do buy this," "If I should take this," "I really should wait."

That "really should wait" means, "I don't intend to wait, but maybe I really should." While he is saying that, the buyer is looking at you and waiting for you to say something, anything, that will help him to talk himself out of the deal. Actually, this is the time to do everything possible to help him to make a decision.

Another approach sometimes used by aggressive salesmen is to have the contract filled out in advance. It is difficult, but this technique may help:

Pick up the contract and make a gesture as though you are about to hand it to the prospect. If he reaches for it, takes it, you have made a deal. If he resists, saying, "I'm not ready for that now," you have not lost anything. Keep on selling.

When you get a good buying signal, close immediately. Don't wait. Don't even finish your previous sentence. Just close!

Our Buying Signal Skit

Let's demonstrate how some buying signals are overlooked in this small skit.

A lady customer, who is familiar with a house that is on the market, enters the real estate office and confronts the salesman:

"I want to buy the house on Woodland Drive that you showed us," she announces.

The salesman is happy. He fills out the contract and gets her signature. Now he is supposed to go to her house that evening and get her husband's signature.

Hubby calls that night and says he will stop at the realty office.

"No, no, no," Big Leaguer insists. "I want to come to your home because I want to see what it is like, anyway."

"Well, hurry," the husband pleads. "I have an important meeting with my company and I should be there now."

Big Leaguer arrives at the buyers' home a half hour later and this is what ensues:

Salesman: "Good evening, Mr. Grant."

Buyer: "Hello. My wife says you have brought a contract for me to sign. Have you got it with you?"

Salesman: "Yes, but I will get to that. First, I want to tell you about this really gorgeous new home that you are buying."

Buyer: "I know all about it. We have friends who lived there. We have been in the house maybe 40 times."

Salesman: "Yes, but knowing a friend doesn't mean you know everything about his home. You know, for instance, it is not in a declining neighborhood. I thought I would mention that."

Buyer: "We are well aware of that."

Salesman: "You do know it?"

Buyer: "Certainly."

Salesman: "I see. The way I feel about it when I sell a house to somebody, my conscience would bother me if I didn't tell the customer all the details about the house and what they should expect."

Buyer: "Good. Now I am in a bit of a hurry. Do you have the contract?"

Salesman: "Please. Let's not rush into this. I have to tell you a few things about the property, or I won't be able to sleep tonight. All right? Now when this freeway comes through, it will take off the back end of your garage, but if you have a compact car you will be O.K. Besides, the freeway is going to help because it will give you a nice big road between you and your neighbors . . . ."

Buyer: "I understand, but I am in a hurry!"

Salesman: "Hey! Hold it a minute. O.K.? It is my time, too, you know. Anyway, let's consider the basement. They probably told you about the basement; your friends, I mean. They told you it didn't leak or anything?"

Buyer: "Yeah."

Salesman: "Well, it doesn't. Just when it rains. So, anyhow, you said you have to go somewhere?"

Buyer: "I sure did."

Salesman: "All right. Just a few more minutes then. I will explain all this to you. I understand your daughter is a model."

Buyer: "Yes."

Salesman: "They tell me she is pretty sharp. You've got only about four blocks to a bus stop. That will give her some exercise walking back and forth."

Buyer: "Four blocks?"

Salesman: "See. I told you there is a lot of stuff about this property that you didn't know. But four blocks isn't too far. You are sure you want to sign this now?"

Buyer: "Yes! And that is not all I would like to do!"

Salesman: "I don't understand."

Buyer: "You are *so* right!"

If you call yourself a salesman, I certainly hope you noticed the buying signals better than our Big Leaguer did in the skit above.

How to Raise the Buyer's Offer

Assume the price of a home is $20,000. You don't tell any prospect that the "asking price" is $20,000. You say, "it is $20,000."

The buyer says, "I'll offer $18,000 and that is all."

You must have a positive attitude and control the situation. Once you lose control, you are dead. So say, "Eighteen thousand, I know the seller won't accept. But suppose he would come down to $19,500. Would you go up to $19,500?"

Some prospects will say, "No, $18,000. I'd go up to $18,500, but try to get it for $18,000."

Keep counseling them until they commit themselves.

Salesman: "Oh, $18,500? You want this house, don't you? I mean, I want to get it for you at the best possible price. I am on your side. But the idea is that you have to give me a fair fighting chance. Let's not aggravate the seller. If you aggravate the seller and I try to get him to agree to a low offer, he will be completely unreasonable. He won't give you a decent counter offer. In fact, he might not even want to sell to you.

"I want to get this home for you and to help you, so say the seller will take $19,500. You are going to $18,500. So just split the difference."

Buyer: "Oh, no!"

Salesman: "Well, I mean, you are the boss. I'll do anything you tell me." (Stay in there like a boxer and keep punching.) "Listen, what would you say if the seller will come down to $19,250? Would you then be willing to go up to $19,250?

Buyer: "No, I wouldn't. $18,500. That's it!"

Salesman: "Look, I want to get that home for you, but another salesman comes in with a slightly higher offer and we are knocked out of the ballgame. Let me ask, would you lose it for a mere $250? That is only a dollar or two more for the payments. Are you going to lose it for so little? Your wife loves it. Make her happy and buy it for her. Your family will be so happy."

Often the prospect will say, "All right, add $250 more. Make it $18,750 and that's definitely all!"

It is surprising how often that little extra $200 or $300 will settle a deal. Get all offers with an extra $50. The $50 is most important.

When you present an offer with a price that ends in "50" instead of merely being rounded out to the nearest hundred dollars, the seller will think you really worked hard; that you squeezed every last cent you could get out of the buyer. This is the way the professional salesman must operate. The more sales you get, the more money you make.

As soon as you get a contract signed, tell the buyer, "Say a prayer for me."

After you get that contract, have another salesman call the seller and tell him, "Mr. Roberts is on the phone and he has an interested buyer. He wants to come over and see you as soon as he is through. He is busy right now."

"What does he have?" the seller probably will ask. "How much is the offer?"

Your go-between says, "I don't know. He just called me and said he has something important to discuss with you."

The foregoing routine is vital to your future success. If you call the seller direct, he will immediately want to know how much of an offer you have. Commit yourself and he might say not to bother; that he doesn't want the deal. Therefore, let someone else—a go-between—arrange the appointment.

Nor should you wait for a couple of days to close the sale. Remember, the buyer might change his mind.

Handling Fear Successfully

A problem for each buyer or seller is fear. He wonders if he is doing the right thing. Therefore, be very sure to say, each time a buyer or seller signs a contract, "You have made an excellent decision!"

Why is that important? Because your client will go home, worry about the sale and then call you, saying, "I want to look at the home again. I am not sure." Then you can remind him:

"You have made an excellent decision, but you won't realize how wonderful your decision is until about six months from now when the joy of your act will be much greater than you ever dreamed it would be." (Memorize this!)

In the event that you must assure a prospect that he is saving money, multiply the amount by ten and talk in terms of ten years. Don't tell him he will save $100 a year. Rather, tell him that in ten years he will save $1000.

Another important point is to repeat to each buyer when you hand him that contract, "Nobody in town could get it for less!"

Make that part of your finale—the last statement as you leave. For example, "Congratulations! You are using good judgment. Six months from now you are going to enjoy this more than you ever dreamed you would. I want to say one thing, friends; nobody in town could ever have bought this property for even a nickel less. Thank you!" Then beat it, because it is only human for a person to wonder if he paid too much.

Five-Point Closing Plan

Make a copy of the following five-point closing plan and study it well.

1. MINOR POINT CHOICE or ASSUMPTIVE CLOSE
   A. Assume your buyer is going to buy the home shown.
   B. Avoid a firm "No" by offering him a choice between two relatively unimportant details. Example: Do you wish to move immediately upon transfer of the property, or should we allow the seller 30 days possession at $3.00 per day rent to you?
   C. Expect questions, objections, or delays in decision making.

2. SUMMARY CLOSE
   A. With the prospect, list "Reasons for Buying" in one column and "Ideas Against Buying" in another column of a "T" (trial) close.
   B Ask for a decision based on many "Yeses" listed.
   C. If he still holds back, probe for the "Real Reason" for not buying. Example: fear, right move, etc.

3. CASH IN ON OBJECTIONS
   A. Listen for clues as to why he can not act. Use, "others have told us a convenience loan was terrific," etc.
   B. Ask him to buy, using his objection for a hinge. Example: Need a paint job, however that is good because you can paint it the way you like it.

4. PENALTY AND PROFIT

   A. Point out danger in delay—another salesman might teletype deal while the prospect hesitates.

   B. Give emotional appeals to strengthen his ideas.

   C. Reassure him—That no one would ever find a better buy—and what a smart move he is making.

5. SILENCE

   A. Remember after logic, emotional appeal and assurance of a smart move—SILENCE— because the first one who speaks LOSES!

   B. Anticipate that he might blow off steam which merely indicates that he lost. Ask: Do you want the mirror to stay? Or, Do you wish to move after school is out? Sign here.

Chapter Thirteen

Closing the Seller

Take your signed offer and get to your seller as quickly as possible. Walk in and begin the greetings:

"Mr. Ramsey, meet Mr. Wilson, a fellow salesman. He drove me here tonight because my car has been acting up. I have something important to talk to you about."

Always sit down at the kitchen or dining room table and spend a moment or two discussing some pleasantry. Make sure you have a solid, legal contract backed up with a substantial note or down payment before you present it to the seller. You will be reversing your closing when you talk to the seller. First, you will be talking about the "to do's" of the negotiations.

"I have this buyer who wants to move in 30 days after transfer of title. How does that suit you? Is that adequate time to move, do you think? They would like the draperies."

Once you eliminate these problems, work on price by telling the seller the "fight story."*

"This buyer tells me he has seen so many homes that he feels he is an expert.

"He feels that he knows more about the market value than I do. That's the attitude this buyer has. He was tough! He gave me an $18,000 offer."

Watch the sellers reaction to that statement. You must watch the expression to judge the seller's reaction. Some sellers

---

*"Fight Story" excerpts from: *Brass Tacks of Real Estate Selling,* by Ray Smith, 310 Arballo Drive, San Francisco. Copyright 1955 by Ray Smith.

are tough. Some are meek. The meek ones say, "Boy, am I going to give it to them." But if you are dealing with the tough ones, brace yourself.

When you tell sellers the sizes of the offers, they frequently start ranting and raving. They are angry and they kick things or vent their fury in similar ways. Just sit there and watch them quietly. Then say:

"Wait a moment. Let me explain. I didn't finish.

"I wouldn't write it up for $18,000. I talked to this buyer. I said to him, 'You know the price of this home is $20,000. Let's assume the seller would come down to $19,500. Would you go up to $19,500?'

"He said that he absolutely wouldn't, but he admitted that he would go up as high as $18,500. I tried then for $19,250. Again he refused to budge, or even split the difference. When I told him he would have to go higher and he said no, I asked him, 'Would you lose it for $250?' So, finally, the buyer consented to $18,750.

"Here it is, Mr. Lane. I wish I could have produced more for you, but I fought all the way. I got him up from $18,000 to $18,750. This buyer has $4000 down with no second mortgage to you. It is 99% sure that it will go through."

Most sellers will go through that pitch again. They will say:

"No, I won't take that $18,750."

"You are the boss. I am only explaining to you. Whatever you tell us, we will do. I am on your side."

"No. Go back and get more. I won't take $18,750."

You must stick to your guns! You must stop that clock. When the seller says, "No!" that's the time you go to work. Believe me, that is the only time when you really go to work. Tell your seller:

"See this purchase agreement? Right now, it is only a piece of paper. Once you sign this, the buyer has bought himself a home.

"But during the time you are refusing to sign it, he could be riding by with his relatives. He could be pointing out your home and be saying, 'This is the one I am thinking of buying.' They could be telling him that he is foolish for buying this one; that there is a new one nearby on which he could be making a better buy. There goes our sale!

"I remember another occasion just like this when I was at the seller's home and he was stalling on the signing. You know, the phone rang and the seller answered it and said it was for me. So I got on the phone and my gosh, it was the buyer. 'Did you get the home for me yet?' he asked. L told him no. He said, 'Forget about it. I've found a better home and I'm going to take it.' So I lost a sale and the seller lost a buyer."

Emphasize the fact that once the seller signs, the prospect has bought and can't back out. If the seller still wants to fight, you can continue with:

"We have two buyers for this home. We have two and one is for $18,750." (Keep the purchase agreement in your hand.) "We have you and this fellow who is giving you $18,750. You turn this offer down and you are buying this home for $18,750. You can't have both. If I walk out of here, they're going to think you bought it for $18,750. So you can't have both." (Of course, they may still fight.)

"For the 45 days that we have had this listing, you have been a seller. But now we have a legal contract and a substantial deposit. As a seller, your selling is going to end tonight because you are now assuming the role of a buyer. If you turn down this offer for $18,750, it means that you are buying this home for $18,750.

"I hope you are not buying it back for $18,750 with the idea that you can make a couple of hundred dollars. Because if you want to work as a speculator, I can get you a couple of homes that you can clean up and possibly make a few hundred dollars. So why gamble for $200 on your own place?"

Put small bits of paper in a pile. Make a big pile and a little pile. Ask your seller if he will play cards with you and gamble with that big pile.

"Imagine, $18,750 against my $200. I said, would you gamble? The most you can win from me is $200. If I lost $200, it wouldn't even upset me. I wouldn't lose sleep over it. Lose $18,750 and I probably would put a noose around my neck."

Keep sticking with them. A seller always has two prices in mind; an asking price and a realistic price that he and his wife had discussed.

"What was your bottom price?"

"To tell the truth, our bottom price was $19,250."

"$19,250? Then that other price was just an asking price. The real price is $19,250. We've got a buyer for $18,750. Five hundred dollars apart! Would you lose this buyer for $500? Maybe you can get another buyer with a couple of hundred dollars more and maybe not.

"I am on your side and I want to help, but I have to understand something. Would you make any compromise at all?"

Sometimes the seller will admit that he will agree to a compromise of a few hundred dollars. In the above situation, he might be willing to get his price down to $19,000. Then you are close! Tell him you will do anything he wants you to do, but explain that any change he makes in the purchase agreement gives the buyer a loophole to say, "I don't want this house."

Then, relieve the pressure by changing the subject a bit. You must give the seller time to think. Perhaps he will say, "Oh, well, I guess I'll take it." If not, field this question and the following argument to him:

"Would you buy it? Let's assume I had you as a prospect and I showed you a couple of my homes. We ride around and look at other houses and I pull in front, here. Would you buy this house for $18,750?

"A lady once told me, 'Wait a minute. I am going to call my brother.' She picked up the phone and said, 'Joe, would you pay $15,000 for my three-family house on 65th St.?' He answered, 'No!' She came back and said, 'Where do I sign?' "

Often the seller will reply, "No, I wouldn't pay that much for this house." You have him!

But if the seller keeps fighting, give him some more pitches. If you keep striving, you will outlast him because it is that second, third or fourth hour when he weakens. Sometimes when you go that long, the seller's wife will interrupt, saying, "Come on, it is getting late and we want to go to bed. You better finish this tomorrow." Just relax a little more and keep talking.

"Do you want me to go back for that additional sum?" you ask the seller.

"Sure," he answers.

"Are you sure you do? Really? Would you put in writing that six months from now, in the event the buyer wants to sell, he can get all of his money back?"

"I can't guarantee that he'll get his money back!"

"Right! You would be foolish to go along with such a condition. You already have him by the neck, so don't lose him."

It is extremely important to remember that you must relieve the tension when it reaches a climax. The reason you do this, of course, is to give your seller an opportunity to think. You can not close a transaction and lock the sellers in 10 or 15 minutes because there is too much money involved. You are dealing with his entire life and all of his savings. This is serious! If he makes a bum decision now, someday he may want you to justify it.

Consider, for example, that no matter how much the sale is—$18,000, $25,000, $40,000—you are asking the client to assume a relatively heavy obligation for about 20 years or more. The magnitude of the transaction weighs just as heavily on the seller, and particularly so if he is moving up to a better home and needs every penny he can get out of his old house.

Can you, then, expect him to make a decision in 10 or 15 minutes? He has to say "No, and beat it." And just about everything else. But what is he really saying? He means: "I am not sure in my mind. Help me." Sure, he won't say in front of his wife, "I don't know. Help me, real estate man." That would make him look very small.

Pride always governs our reactions. Animals react by using a defensive mechanism. So does man. Your seller's mechanism is: "Go back for more money!" It means: "I am not sure."

The seller and his wife will say, "We don't want to sell at that price. We should get more. It is a lovely house." They are using a defensive mechanism. They want more time to think.

Help them to think. Relieve the tension. Switch the conversation to their children, or to their hobbies. Then come back with the pressure. You must understand this on-again, off-again tension and pressure is your normal procedure. Don't expect quick or easy closes.

The average real estate man, I submit, responds this way.

The seller blows his top. The salesman says to himself, the seller is not interested . . . he is angry!

Actually, the seller is not angry. All he wants is to tell you indirectly, "I need more time to think. Convince me. Please help me!" He won't put his thoughts into words because, at this time, he is not sure that you are on his side. So let him think.

Your seller is not a genius, either. He may have a high I.Q. Possibly he is a college graduate. It still doesn't mean a thing in this instance. All persons are capable of being slow, plodding thinkers when it comes to real estate. You have to give them time to analyze and think.

Frequently, people demand quick decisions from their relatives and friends; from the public in general or brokers in particular. You have to realize that the other person is not thinking as fast as you are. He is on more unfamiliar ground. He will need more time to make a judgment and to arrive at what appears to you to be a perfectly obvious answer.

On one closing, the sellers were undecided as to whether or not they should take the offer. They insisted that I leave the contract and see them again the following day. Instead, I said I would go to the corner shop for a cup of coffee and come back in 15 minutes. When the 15 minutes were up, I went back and they greeted me with, "We will take the offer!"

By walking away, I relieved the tension and gave them an opportunity to discuss the offer privately. I knew I did not want to wait until the following day, but merely give them time to reach a decision.

A husband and a wife usually won't make any concessions in front of a stranger. Give them a little time alone and they will inquire of each other: "What do you think, honey? Don't you think maybe we should take the offer?" The sellers actually are closing themselves while the salesman is gone for 15 minutes. Don't put them on the spot where they must make a difficult decision and do it fast.

Paid $5000 to Be Healthy

Whenever the husband or wife is ailing, tell this story about a man who was ill:

The man went to many doctors, none of whom could cure him. He was so desperate he did not know what to do. About ready to give up, he said, "I'll try one more doctor." This final doctor said, "I can cure you."

Our ill friend was amazed.

"You can cure me?" he pursued.

"Yes I can, but it is going to cost you $5000."

"Five thousand dollars? Are you crazy, doctor? I am going to pay you $5000?"

"You want to get cured, don't you?"

"Of course."

"So hand over the $5000."

"Doctor, where are the pills and the medicines that the other doctors gave me?"

"I am not going to prescribe any pills or medicines."

"Doctor, you are different."

"That is right. From now on, whenever you have any problem, I want you to say, 'I don't care.' Understand? You don't have any more complaints or worries. That is why you paid me $5000."

So the man went out into the world and whenever a problem arose, he said to himself, "I don't care." You know, his health improved; his business picked up.

Likewise, Mr. Lane, say, "I don't care" and put your name right here.

A Snowy Approach

Before going on another close, I remembered the customer had a big, long driveway, some 1000 feet long and 12 feet wide. The previous winter we had some huge snowfalls and I had made pictures of four and five-foot high snow drifts. I took these photos with me when I went to the seller's home and I observed, "If the buyer comes here, tomorrow, and sees big drifts like these in your driveway, the sale will be lost."

The seller remembered the snow. He knew what I meant and he signed without further hesitation.

It is important that you get a seller to make an early decision. Tell him that while you and he are discussing the offer, the buyer's uncles and aunts could be riding by the house; that these are well-intentioned people who will tell him that he is wrong; that the house is overpriced, and that they know where he can find a much better buy for his money.

There should be time to think. Yes, but not so much time that the sale will be jeopardized. You want action and signatures.

When tension has reached the popping point, it is a good idea to ask for a glass of water, or perhaps suggest a cup of coffee. Again, that will decelerate the tension and give the seller time to think and to make a favorable decision.

Overcoming Commission Cuts

How to overcome the request to cut a commission? Use four pitches.

Answer No. 1:

Frequently, a seller will say, "How about cutting the commission?" Give a slight smile and say, "I know one real estate company that had 40 salesmen and five offices. It went out of business. An auditor checked its books and found out that it was working on a 4% basis. That is why it couldn't exist. To sell homes, we must have ample advertising. Our company does have it. We invest $5000 a month in newspaper advertising alone. Our salesmen make 60% of the commission. The company, of course, gets 40%, but with that 40%, the company has to pay all of the expenses."

The seller says, "Well, you can cut a little commission." To which you reply, "The truth is that I can't cut a commission. We are not allowed to do that because we would get fired."

Answer No. 2:

How about cutting commission? Smile nicely and say, "I never thought of it." Pause. "There only is one problem. If I were to cut a commission, it probably would be all right with my company because one deal isn't that important. You are nice people. It isn't that one deal that matters. When I go back to the office and say I cut a commission, the boss would probably overlook it. He would say, 'That's all right.' The other salesmen would hear that and they would all want to cut commissions. So the boss would have to fire me. If I went out for another job, nobody would hire me because I would then be known as a commission cutter. You don't want me to get fired. This is my bread and butter."

Answer No. 3:

You want to convey to the seller that you are being fair to everybody.

"We don't cut for anyone. They all get the same fair treatment. It would be unfair if we were to cut a commission for you. So in order to be fair to all of our sellers, we cut for no one. We want to be just as fair with you. We charge the same rate to everybody. No favorites. We like you, too."

You can turn this argument around another way as follows:

"Are you satisfied that we have done a fairly good job? I know you work hard. Suppose you went to get your next pay check and the boss said, 'You did a swell job, but my wife bought a coat this week so I had to take some of your money to pay for that coat!' You would not want the boss to lower your pay after you had done your work. We have done our job. Now we would like to get paid in full."

Answer No. 4:

The seller says, "You had the house listed just three days and you want a thousand dollars commission. Do you feel justified—three days and a thousand bucks?"

You reply: "I had a tooth killing me once. I mean it was painful. I went to a specialist. Three seconds and out it came. He gave me a bill for $20. I said, 'Twenty dollars to pull a tooth? It took only three seconds.' He said, 'Well, next time you have a bad tooth, I will do 15 minutes of pulling.' I told him to forget it. The three seconds were just fine. The same is true with your house. You won't have people trooping through it. Your home is sold! Would you really want us to take longer to sell your home?"

When the seller really is fighting you about the price or the commission, dramatize the situation. Pretend to be looking into a crystal ball and say, "I don't know where the next buyer is coming from. If I had a crystal ball here I could tell you, but I just don't know."

You have to prove to him that he is getting his money's worth. That is the important thing!

This also is a good spot for the reverse answer to his objections. When he says, "Your company charges me 7% and I could have given it to another company for only a 5% charge," you can offer this answer:

"That is the very reason you gave the listing to our company; because we do charge 7%. And others have paid us this amount, too, because they knew—as I am sure you know—that our company does much more for you. The firms who charge 5% can afford to do so because they don't do as thorough or as effective a job.

"I imagine you also could say you buy your clothes, food and other necessities from companies who charge a fair price. Again, you probably could get these items for less if you would search for low-cost outlets to patronize.

"If a man had a cow in the backyard, he could give you a quart of milk for less money. I am quite sure that isn't what you want. You want to pay a fair price and get value.

"Sure, some will cut commissions, but each company and each man knows his own worth. I am worth 7%. People will pay a fair price."

Tell the story about the seller who refused an offer. He was transferred and had to move out of town. The refusal of the offer almost caused a divorce in the family. One party wanted to take the offer. The other party refused it. The home sat vacant for more than a year and eventually was sold for $2000 less than the price that originally was offered. This is one of many instances in which delayed action resulted in less money.

Here is another example. The prospect offered the seller $28,000 for a given house before it was listed by us. The seller had rejected that offer and subsequently, we had the house on the market for about four months. The prospect showed up again with a $26,000 offer which the seller accepted. The seller told us he was afraid to refuse the new offer because he might lose even more money.

We had a sale in which the fellow (the seller) was out of

town. He was a cook. His wife was here, in our city. Their house
had been listed for sale for $20,900 through two exclusives
before we got it, but with no break in price. Finally we had an
offer and stepped in to try and close it. The lady said her
husband was a chef in a well-known hotel in Florida. The real
close on this woman was the fact that our salesman, who had
been a guest in that Florida hotel, remarked, "Oh, that is a
beautiful hotel! And I must say, I never saw such beautiful
chorus girls in all my life!"

The salesman planted the thought in that girl's mind that
her man just might be living it up in Florida while she was
babysitting with an overpriced house. She telephoned him
immediately and said, "You are going to take this $19,000
offer." And he did.

Let us say you have an $18,900 home and you get an
$18,300 offer. On all contracts insist on that extra $50. Then,
with an $18,350 offer, it is easier to convince the seller that he
is getting every penny available; that you really fought for him.

Even the banker will be impressed with that extra ginger-
bread. Don't kid about it, saying my buyers might pay more.
Go into that close with what you sincerely believe is the best
possible offer.

In short, you can't get a dime more! If the seller refuses
this offer, the deal is dead.

Some salesmen panic. They want to have a cushion. But
nobody can work effectively on closing the seller if he presents
an if-come offer to that seller.

Could you possibly consider going to the seller with an
undesirable offer when you know that the buyer is ready,
willing and able to put more money into the deal? If you were
the seller, you wouldn't want that to happen to you. And the
salesman who is willing to be a carrying pigeon for anemic,
mediocre offers should be jolted out of the business!

Be honest. "This is all I have; please analyze it," you
inform the seller. Don't go to him with a fairy tale. Let's have
the best offer and none of that baloney about what the buyer
will come up with.

Too often, on a close, the salesman is ready to jump up
and run back for an extra fifty bucks because he thinks he can

do it. Truthfully, he should not leave. He should have gone into that close so prepared that his very manner implies, "Refuse this offer and there is no possible deal."

If you are honest with yourself and with your seller, you will have more satisfaction on the closing.

In recognizing that you might spend three or four hours in closing the seller, I think you would be well-advised to spend an equal amount of time with the buyer, in trying to get the highest possible offer in writing. Sometimes that extra effort on your part will make the difference between a sale or a dud. You must be fair with both buyers and sellers.

The Final Step

Return a contract immediately upon obtaining the sellers' signatures.

I think there is a tendency in most of our real estate offices to feel that God is going to help us and protect us until the following morning from customers who change their minds. I think you should realize that maybe God is working on something else than real estate projects this month.

So, even if it is 10 p.m., 11 p.m., or midnight, you should go to that buyer's door and say, "I just came from the seller." It will impress the buyer. He will be thinking, "This salesman has been working for me this long! Why should I complain that he is interrupting my slumbers. I couldn't actually sleep anyway, I was so worried."

Never procrastinate or become negligent just because you have made a deal and it is past 9 p.m. Don't assume that it is all right to go home; that you can deliver the contract tomorrow, or give the buyer a copy in the bank. This type of thinking does not cement the sale, nor give the buyer positive assurance that he has bought a home. Return the signed copy and leave immediately.

When you are returning that signed contract or signed counter-offer to the buyer, give him the fight story again, only in reverse.

"Nobody else in town can get it for less. The reason I didn't come back with a verbal $19,200 is because my feeling is that you want the house. I feel you would not want to lose it for a mere $400. So I made sure I had this counter offer in writing so that the seller can't change his mind. If you just initial this contract, the home is yours! It is only a dollar more a month on the payments. Your wife loves it. Nice community. All your friends will envy you living in that neighborhood. You will be happy living there. Just initial it here."

Chapter Fourteen

Finding Prospects for Trade-Ins

The person who is most susceptible to trading, I have found, is a person who has had his home for sale for many months, possibly for even a year. He is more susceptible to a trade-in plan than anybody else. When you walk in to list his home, ask: "How about a trade?"

The reaction of such a seller usually is, "A trade? Oh, boy, I'll get this dog off my hands once and for all."

Some Ideas on Trading and Prospects

Here is an example of a trade. The seller had a house on the market for nine months. He and his wife were a middle-aged couple. They paid a premium price for the house when they bought it. During the four years they lived in it, they installed aluminum siding and a brick front, adding about $2200 to their investment. Yet, they did not want to lose too much money, which they would be doing if I listed it for $18,900.

So I asked them what they wanted to buy. They told me a brick ranch. I knew of a building lot, so I asked, "How about Darlington Ave? First lot from the corner. Close to transportation."

They were excited. They inspected the lot and were even

more excited when I visited them the next day. In the
meantime, I checked a builder who told me he could build the
brick ranch for $23,500. I needed a $1500 cushion to work
with and quoted a price of $25,500.

Now the buyers said they wanted a garage. So I threw in
the garage for $500. In fact, I said, $25,500 for house, garage
and sod on the front. They were happy.

They paid $25,500 and the builder returned the $1500
cushion so we could take the former home on trade. What a
tremendous deal this was, getting $1500 plus the commission.
That is $3030 in commissions. The buyer paid us $1000 for
buying his old home at $18,000. In effect, we were buying the
home at $17,000. We had a $1500 cushion to work with, so
actually, we paid $15,500 for the house. It was sold a month
later at a profit of $2000.

Over the years, my sales team has developed a list of 17
sources of prospects. We have this list posted in our offices so
that all of our new salesmen can be exposed to it as quickly as
possible.

The list is published here as a bonus benefit for the readers
of this book.

Seventeen Sources of Prospects

1. *Bird Dogs:* A tried and true method. You should have
four to six good bird dogs working for you. Personnel managers,
postmen, milkmen, store clerks, housewives, union officials, and
policemen are your best bird dogs.

2. *Our Former Buyers:* Use the "Sold Book" to call and
get acquainted (or re-acquainted). Ask how they are getting
along. Ask them to bird-dog for you. Get their friends' names
and "cold canvass" their friends. You have an invaluable
introduction.

3. *People in Vicinity of Houses for Sale:* Visit all the
people to whom you sent a "Choose Your Neighbor" letter.
Leave a pen and your card at each visit. Ask for names of
people they know who want to sell or buy.

4. *Renters' Letters:* Send list of "Best Buys of the Week"
to tenants in all apartments in your area of operation. Better

yet, go to them. Don't wait for them to come to you. How long has it been since you personally have canvassed a group of apartments?

5. *New Home Salesman:* Tract salesmen in your territory should be contacted for referrals. These men make very good bird dogs. They are licensed and can be paid a referral fee upon completion of a sale.

6. *Prospect Card File:* Your old prospects should be contacted by telephone regarding your "Best Buy of the Week" list. There is gold in the files of prospects' names that are a year or more old. Go through these files and call—all of them!

7. *Open Houses:* A good source of present and future prospects are the persons looking through an "open house." These persons may not like the house being exhibited, but they may be interested in other properties listed by your company. Always get the name and telephone number. Also, copy the license plate number (the Auto Club furnishes the owner's name) and call them.

8. *Trailer Camp:* This is a good source of prospects. Mail your cards and the "Best Buy" list and say, "Trade your trailer for a real home. Enjoy life with comfort."

9. *Owners with Property for Sale:* Ask if they know anyone who might be interested in the property. Ask them to list, of course. Ask them for names of prospects who looked at their place, but who said they were looking for something with less money down, cheaper, etc., and then call on those prospects. Always stop at each "for sale by owner" house and talk. Talk trade. Talk buy. Talk list.

10. *Your Business Cards:* Write your Best Buy on at least 50 of your business cards each week and leave them wherever you go all week. Get rid of those cards by Saturday noon. This is quick and cheap and will produce prospects.

11. *Newspapers:* Marriage and divorce notices! Contact the newly weds about buying; the divorcing couples about selling. Legal newspapers should be scanned for foreclosures. Also watch local community or suburban newspapers. They report marriages, promotions, babies. Cold-canvass these people by telephone. Congratulate them. Tell them you can solve their housing problems.

12. *Civic Activities, Clubs:* If you are not a "joiner" start joining now. Get into the K. of C., PTA, church groups, Lions, Legion, Chamber of Commerce. Attend meetings. Hand out cards.

13. *Check "Real Estate Wanted" Ads:* Check the real estate-wanted classified advertisements and call about your for-sale houses. Do this with all papers. Telephone advertisers and owners of property for rent. Talk listings!

14. *Free Bulletin boards:* Post your Best-Buy List on free bulletin boards in auto washes, industrial plants and other public areas.

15. *Brokers Outside Your Area:* Get acquainted with brokers in "hot areas" and cooperate with them. They might have buyers from homes in your section which can be listed, or they might have sellers who will be buying in your area.

16. *Other Business Places:* Call on a business nearest your office. Offer to scratch backs. You will send them customers; they will send you prospects. Talk to everyone you buy from about sending you prospects.

17. *Old Appraisals; Expired MLS Pictures:* Ask if you can sell their house so they will have cash to buy another home.

Chapter Fifteen

Home-Buying Tips that Make
Friends and Create Customers

Success, it has been said, can be measured by a man's ability to make friends.

That is especially true in the real estate field. You will get listings and negotiate sales in more or less direct proportion to the number of friends you cultivate.

How do you win over these people? By offering them service and assistance; by extending your hand of friendship. It always is a good idea to distribute business cards. You want people to remember your name. But sometimes it is even better to give prospects something they can use and keep; something which is allied with their interests and your own home sales activities.

For instance, from time to time, small booklets or leaflets are available on real estate subjects. Many of these can be imprinted with your name, address and telephone number, or you can attach your neatly printed, gummed label bearing the same identification.

When you give this helpful information to a future home buyer or home seller, you have better than a fifty-fifty chance of converting that prospect into a customer. Then, watch your income zoom upward!

In Cleveland, we have found that the "How to Buy A Home" booklets written by real estate editor Robert F. Brennan are enthusiastically received by prospective buyers. Brennan, who writes about the real estate business in a clear, chatty, informative way, is a past president of the National Association of Real Estate Editors. Frequently, we make reprints from his booklets, or of his local articles, distributing them to our friends and future customers.

Here, then, are some of the Brennan words to which we like to attach the Rybka name and offer as good reading to that would-be buyer:

THERE'S A HOME IN YOUR FUTURE!*

Home buying has been made easier for all of us!

You might ask: "Is that so? But what about prices? What about all of those strange words and terms? What about those complex forms and papers? And how in the world will I ever pay for a home of my own?"

Have courage, friend. Take comfort from the fact that you are not alone—that practically everybody now owning a home once asked the same questions.

A scant 50 years ago, home ownership seemed like an unattainable dream to most people. Prices were lower, but so were incomes. Moreover, down payments were larger, terms were shorter and interest rates were higher than they are in many places today.

You probably have heard it said that when you buy a home, you are making one of life's biggest investments. That is true. But more Americans are buying more homes each year. Statistics show that instead of buying or building a home for a lifetime, owners are re-selling their homes after nine years.

Whether you purchase a home for a lifetime or a decade, you should enter into the transaction with care and considera-

*This section is an excerpt from the booklet, *How to Buy a Home,* by Robert F. Brennan; published by The Cleveland Press, 1968. Updated editions of Mr. Brennan's home-buying booklets are prepared periodically and sold through the Public Service Department of The Cleveland Press, 901 Lakeside Ave., Cleveland, Ohio.

tion. You may want to sell that home and buy another in 9 to 11 years.

Heed the experts in home sales, real estate law, and financing. They say you will be happier with your home purchase if you investigate thoroughly, get everything in writing and make sure you understand what you are signing. The time spent with a qualified adviser, rather than acting on quick hunches, can save you money.

Which Is the Home for You?

Telling a person what home to buy is like trying to advise a young man on how to choose a wife. Guidelines can be offered, but the decision almost always is made on the grounds of personal taste.

You can choose an existing or used home, a new house built by a developer on his lot, or a home that you can contract to have built on your own lot.

Before deciding which way to go, think about your budget and ask yourself how much use and enjoyment the home will give you.

You might consider that new homes have many glamorous features, modern innovations and the promise of a number of repair-free years at the start.

But the new-home buyer should find out if he will be required to pay any unpaid or future assessments. He also should think about room sizes, landscaping and the cost of items that he may want to install in the home.

In the older home, many improvements may have been made by the previous owner. The condition of the home and neighborhood will be more apparent. However, the buyer usually is required to make a larger down payment. If changes must be made, remember that when you add new space to an older home, you increase the value of the property about 75¢ for every $1 spent. Remodeling—such as modernizing the kitchen—increases the value about 50¢ for every $1 spent.

For both existing homes and new houses, location is of prime importance. A poor location will result in early dissatisfaction with the home and may necessitate selling again.

It may seem elementary, but many people fail to look over the neighborhood before they buy a house. Take a ride around the neighborhood in the daytime. Do it again after dark because neighborhoods have changing characteristics under varying conditions.

Selecting the Site or Neighborhood

In choosing your future neighborhood, it is best to decide upon a general area and then pick the specific location.

If you are building a house, don't plan a 75-foot house for a 70-foot lot. Have the property surveyed to see that there are no encroachments. Beware of lots at bargain prices. There may be a good reason for the low price that will cost you dollars later.

Consider the neighborhood of your choice carefully. Does it offer the environment you want for your family? Do the neighbors appear congenial and are they property owners who will take an interest in maintaining the neighborhood? (Check the back section of the city directory; property owners have a circled "O" following their names.)

Does the neighborhood offer all the facilities you want? Are all the necessary public utilities—water, gas, electricity, sewers, street lights—in and paid? Will your new home be convenient to church, school, amusements, shopping areas and public transportation? Is there a guard at the corner to help your children cross the street? Will you be near a main artery to help the wage-earner to get to and from work?

Make sure that the neighborhood has been zoned for residential use and that it is protected from future business use. See that the location of the home on the lot conforms with the building code. Find out if the home itself conforms with neighborhood restrictions.

While you are looking over the neighborhood, check these: is the home or lot near railroads, airport, noisy highways, open creeks, heavy industry with accompanying noise, smoke or fumes? While you might be willing to live with any one of these, a preponderance or combination of these detracting factors could kill your future happiness and also have a detrimental influence on you home's value.

Does the lot satisfy your needs? Consider more than just its size. Hills, for one thing, have scenic charm, yet they represent an obstacle to a power lawnmower. Trees provide shade and enhance the value of your home in a way that can't be measured in dollars. Curved streets will discourage through-traffic and long blocks will eliminate hazardous intersections.

If you are looking at a model house on a street not yet developed, or if you are contracting to have a house built for you, try to envision what the neighborhood will look like when the other homes are built.

How Do You Get the Money?

The home buyer is lucky. There are many places for him to get that money he needs to buy a home. Cautious lenders prevent him from going overboard in debt for a house that is beyond his means. Furthermore, mortgage loan borrowing is one of the least expensive ways of obtaining money.

You should realize the money you borrow is a commodity, the same as food, soap, clothing or autos. You have to pay for it in the form of an interest charge. And just as the price of food or other items fluctuates according to supply and demand, so does the price of money. These price changes are reflected in varying interest charges and terms.

For many years, lenders said you should not spend more for a home than three times your annual income. Now, the tendency is to be a little more conservative. With conventional financing, a borrower should not spend more for a home than twice his annual income, according to some mortgage bankers.

Another rule of thumb: your monthly earnings should be at least four or five times larger than the amount that will be due each month for interest, principal and taxes. (But be careful; you also will have to pay utility bills, casualty insurance premiums and maintenance costs.)

Savings and loan companies will lend up to 80% of a home's appraised value and, in some cases, make 90% loans. State and national banks are permitted to lend up to 80% of a home's appraised value on terms up to 25 years. Mortgage loans also are made by loan correspondents through their lenders, commercial banks and insurance companies. The insurance companies will make loans up to 75% of appraised value.

The bank appraisal does not necessarily indicate that you are making a good or a bad buy and should not be used as such. The appraisal is usually less than the sale price and is an appraisal for mortgage purposes only. Personal property, such as carpeting and draperies, are not included in the appraisal.

You will be required to make payments over the years, therefore you may choose the institution with which you wish to deal. But don't ignore the suggestions of your builder or broker who probably already has inquired about financing for a particular home and who knows which lender can meet your needs quickly and conveniently.

When you apply for a loan you will find that these three basic types are available:

CONVENTIONAL—A regular loan made in the conventional manner by the financial institution itself and not insured or guaranteed by any governmental agency.

FHA—A loan from a private financial institution that is insured by the Federal Housing Administration. FHA insures the lender against any possible loss through default on the mortgage by the borrower.

VA or GI—A loan that can be made only to a qualified veteran. The Veterans Administration issues a guaranty to the lender covering a portion of the loan.

The FHA and VA loans provide for lower down payments on modest-priced homes. Additional appraisals must be made and more rigid restrictions are imposed because the government must have some control over what it is guaranteeing.

One criticism of these loans is that they take longer to process than does the conventional loan.

Taking That First Step

After you have decided to buy you will have to sign your name seven times before your deal is complete. Your signature is required on the contract, a cognovit note (if any), loan application, mortgage deed, mortgage note, escrow instructions, and a signature card for your lending institution.

The first step is to sign a purchase agreement. This is a contract sometimes referred to as an offer. The contract must be accompanied with earnest money to prove that you are acting in good faith. If you are dealing through a broker, he may ask you to sign a cognovit note, payable on demand, in lieu of a check or cash deposit.

The purchase agreement governs the deal and becomes binding when signed by both buyer and seller. It should clearly state: adequate description and location of property; purchase price; amount of earnest money which is to be applied to purchase price, or returned to buyer if the seller is unable to go through with the deal; additional cash to be deposited in escrow; provision to get mortgage; information about any contingent sale; and provision for chattels, deed, dower rights, title guarantee, escrow fee, possession date and date funds are to be deposited in escrow.

The law says, "let the buyer beware." Therefore, your contract should be definite and complete. It should state that there are no building violations or mechanic's liens and note any easements or restrictions. If the seller is silent and does not tell you about these things, you have no redress.

After the contract has been signed by both buyer and seller, you must both receive copies of it.

You will apply for a loan and be asked for full information about your marital status, number of dependents, place of employment and length of service, plus full particulars about your wife's employment. Appraisal fees are payable with the application.

Before the loan can be approved, an appraiser will investigate the property, photograph the building and make his report to the lending institution, FHA or VA.

If you accept the amount and terms offered by the lender, the note and mortgage must be prepared and signed. If you are married, your spouse must also sign. The lender will state the amount of fire and wind insurance required and will hold the policy while the loan is outstanding.

Sales and purchases are handled through an escrow. Usually the lender also is escrow agent, but the escrow agent could be a title company or lawyer. The seller deposits his deed with the escrow agent with a letter of instructions. If a mortgage loan is involved, the lender deposits the mortgage and mortgage money. The buyer deposits the balance of the purchase price. The escrow agent's function is to protect the interests of the buyer, lender and seller. He acts as an impartial agent to see that the transaction is handled properly. His fee usually is divided between buyer and seller. Amount of the fee is determined by the size of the transaction and the work that is involved.

The title company of your choice receives the mortgage from the bank. It makes a search to see that the title will be good and that there are no liens on the property except the new mortgage. If it is found that there are claims upon the property, the seller will be ordered to pay such claims before a clear title will be given.

The new deed and mortgage are then recorded and title papers, guaranteeing or insuring against defects of title are written for the lender and for you, the new owner.

Another Benefit, Too

The explanations above are just samples of how Bob Brennan guides his readers through the home-buying and home-selling processes. As I said before, we like to reprint these articles and distribute them to our customers.

There also is another benefit, though. In reading such reports by Mr. Brennan and other realty journalists we frequently see ideas that we have overlooked or forgotten. We find, too, forceful expressions which we can incorporate in our bag of sales tools.

I have found that it doesn't pay to miss a trick ... that if you are to be successful in this real estate business, you really must know a lot!

Chapter Sixteen

Guidelines to Keep You On Top!

The salesman's height can be measured with a ruler. His weight can be determined with a scale. But there only is one way to ascertain his worth and that is to judge him by the words and actions he uses to influence his fellow man. This guide to stature, like the common household ruler, is comprised of 12 parts or rules.

Twelve Ways to Win Others to Your Way of Thinking

Rule 1—The only way to get the best of an argument is to avoid it.

You have heard this one before. It is important to avoid arguments. Shun them as much as you would poison. If you win an argument with your prospect, your sales effort is as dead as if you had consumed the poison.

Rule 2—Show respect for the other man's opinions.

In sales work, never tell a man he is wrong. If you imply in any way that your customer is wrong, or if you tell him so, he will seek to defend himself, just as though you had attacked him.

Your attempt to make a point will delay, if not cancel, the agreement you seek. Remember, the Bible says, "agree with thine adversaries quickly."

Rule 3–If you are wrong, admit it immediately and emphatically!

If you do this, your prospect will have greater respect for your sincerity and honesty.

Rule 4–Begin in a friendly way.

Woodrow Wilson was the instigator of the League of Nations and a very peaceful man. Yet he commented, "If you come at me with your fist doubled, I will double mine twice as hard." Isn't it better to talk over the differences than to fight them out?

Rule 5–Get your customer in a "Yes" frame of mind quickly.

It is smarter and easier for you if you get your prospect into the habit of saying "Yes" to some of the minor questions in your sales talk. It will establish an atmosphere of agreement.

You should do this rather than hit him with an important item that may elicit a "No," because he will feel that he must disregard your logic to defend his "No."

Rule 6–Let the other man do a great deal of the talking.

When you let the other man talk, you learn his needs, desires and objections. Then you can concentrate your efforts in presenting the important facts and benefits.

Rule 7–Let the other man feel that the idea is his.

This is a very subtle form of flattery. You are allowing him to build his self image, instead of pushing your own to the forefront.

Rule 8–Try honestly to see things from the other person's viewpoint.

His point of view may be way out of focus as you see the problem, but then you are not in his position. Make a mental switch and you will be more attuned to his situation and have a better understanding of how to put across your own ideas.

Rule 9–Be sympathetic with the other person's ideas and desires because they are very real to him.

Help him to see how he can achieve those ideas and desires and he will resist you less.

Rule 10–Appeal to nobler motives.

Everyone likes to feel that he is the knight in shining armor—a most chivalrous person. If you can appeal to this instinct, your prospect will more than likely try to live up to that ideal.

Rule 11—Dramatize your ideas.

Dramatization in your sales effort will be extremely effective. If your prospect does not agree with an idea, jot it down and literally throw it away.

Rule 12—Evoke a challenge.

I challenge you to memorize these 12 rules because if you do, you always will sell more. In a nutshell, these 12 ideas will help you to get more of that long green stuff.

How to Make Others Like You

Practice these self-help rules and watch your sales soar:

1. Always smile.

Get in the habit of smiling, even when you are using the telephone. They say that the voice with the smile can be conveyed on the telephone. So, on the phone or in person, always smile. Let them know you are a friendly person.

2. Never criticize.

This is difficult to do, especially at home. Right? The natural inclination to criticize can be suppressed though with sufficient practice. Try to restrain yourself consistently in your dealings with your family and co-workers.

We make it a rule in our company, from managers to the lowest man on the totem pole, to refrain from criticizing fellow workers. Instead, we tell the other fellow what a nice job he is doing. We search for the good things and are lavish in our praise. It is a rule that makes everybody stay on their toes as they try to be pleasant and outperform themselves. The result is that our work gives us much more happiness and satisfaction and consequently, it is easier to achieve greater results.

Probably all of us are too quick to criticize one another. Criticism is a form of attack, but as mature, thinking adults, we can't persist in attacking each other. We have to use intelligence and realize it is a waste of time to criticize and/or feel resentment.

Everyone resents being criticized in print or in speech. Consider the man who shot a policeman. Even as he languishes in jail, he says to himself, "In my own heart, I think I acted in self defense." This is another example of how futile it is to criticize. You never can really convince the other person that he is wrong. Dutch Schultz thought he was a public benefactor, not a criminal. Al Capone felt that he was doing people a service by selling them liquor.

Better try to act like Lincoln and overlook the obvious faults.

3. The greatest word and sweetest sound is a person's own name.

More important to an individual than almost anything else is the opportunity to hear his name used and pronounced properly. Be aware of this, always, when you deal with the public. And be sure that you are pronouncing all names correctly.

4. Be a good listener.

Again, there is a natural inclination to talk, but if you would have others like you, let them talk. Moreover, become seriously interested in what they are saying. No matter how humble the other man's background, or how insignificant his calling, be attentive and show respect.

If you are talking, don't monopolize the conversation with talk about yourself or your company. Talk to the public. Talk about them. Make these people feel important and appreciated. They soon enough will know who you are and they will like you much better.

And remember, you can make the other fellow feel important and appreciated. When he comes into your office, don't wait for him to come to you, but stand up and approach him with a greeting. Say, "Thank you for coming in, Mr. Harrison. We are happy you chose our company. This is a wise decision because so many people come here and they all are happy. I am so grateful you came. How may I help you? Please sit down so I can get to know you."

Find out the type of furniture the prospect owns, where they live, facts about their children, their hobbies and desires. Get cozy with them. This will knock out other real estate companies. Frequently, salesmen say their buyers went some place else. Why? Because somebody else made them feel just a little bit better, or more important.

So, when a buyer comes to you, no matter how uninteresting he may seem, make him feel good. If he is in the market for nothing better than a $6400 house, let him know you value his business just as much as the business of a $100,000 home buyer.

Test yourself. Ask yourself, would you treat the person looking at a $7000 home with the same kindness and courtesy as you would show a man buying a $50,000 home? The probable answer is "no" and that is wrong. You have to impress in your own mind that all people are to be shown equal importance and appreciation. This is your responsibility and if you practice it well, it will help you to get referrals and to be a successful person.

Along the same line, this is why you must call your sellers every week; to show your appreciation and interest and to let them feel important. I tell my salesmen to call their sellers every Wednesday; to make this a habit.

When you demonstrate to the other person that you appreciate his interest in you, he marks you as a cultured person. He is happy to be doing business with somebody he can respect. Strangely enough, your kindness and courtesy will have a boomerang effect. In trying to make life more pleasant for others, you will be growing into a finer person with elevated goals and a sincere desire for continued self improvement.

There is an example, here, in the entertainer who performs exceptionally well because he is grateful that a large audience came to see his act. Should you do less? Shouldn't you jump up and be eager to serve, showing your customer that you welcome the opportunity he is presenting to you?

Take a tip from the entertainer. When the buyer walks in, bounce out of your chair and greet him with a sincere, welcoming flourish. Ask questions and let him know he is important.

Everybody Wants to Feel Important

People buy the latest clothes and purchase the biggest homes.

An example: A family of two with six bathrooms (Honest!). No need for all of those rooms, but it is a sign of prestige. It gives the husband and wife a feeling of importance.

In your selling, make your prospects feel important. Keep repeating that it is important. Do so until it is ingrained in your habits. Make everybody feel important.

Sigmund Freud said that the two basic motivations of human nature are the sex urge and the quest for acknowledgement. Today, political scientists say politicians are honest and do a good job because they want to feel important and avoid criticism. This same desire for recognition and respect also is de-emphasizing the theory that people avoid breaking laws because of the threat of jail.

It should be self evident, then, that in showing interest, respect and appreciation, you have a powerful tool that can make the buyer and seller work for you. Once you have mastered the art of making others work for you, you will have reached the first plateau of $16,000 a year. More important, you will be poised for that giant step to an even greater, more satisfying, more successful future.

I know you can do it. Your family knows you can do it. Should you have any less faith in yourself?

You might say, "But, Ed, you haven't spelled out a great system with a bunch of secret rules."

You would be right. There is no magic key to success. Rather, it calls for the recognition of proper application of the basic principles of human nature.

Skim through the foregoing chapters again. You will find some important passages that you will want to underscore and remember. Then make these ideas and suggestions a part of your sales kit. Be assured that they are the principles of human nature.

After you have put these principles to work for a year, you will find that you face your career with far greater confidence.

Chapter Seventeen

Job Description for a Rybka Salesman

The following is an exact copy of the duties and instructions given to each salesman upon joining Rybka Realty. Note that it is in the form of an agreement which must be read and signed by both the salesman and the broker.

Job Description*

The first thing for you to do as a real estate salesman is to set your goal. We mean to actually set down on paper what you expect to do in this job as far as earning money is concerned. You must have a road map if you are going to take a trip through this job. After you have decided how much you want to make, your manager can then help you with a plan to accomplish this goal. This is a "commission job" by choice. It would be simple to pay a salary for the job of selling real estate, but it would be impossible to keep a man of the intelligence, fortitude, and creativity it requires to sell real estate on this basis. There is absolutely no limit to the amount of money that you can make by selling real estate.

One point that we should make clear at the outset is that

---

*Excerpt from the pamphlet: *A Job Description for Real Estate Salesmen,* by Bob Bale; published by Bob Bale Institute, 4710 N. 16th St., Phoenix, Arizona.

in this office the fact that you are on a commission does not mean that you are here to work when and how you want to. We have definite standard procedures which we know get results. You are expected to follow these procedures. We are a company of producing people. After you have gone through your basic training and are out in the field operating on your own, we must have a sale from you every month without exception. We must have individual production on a monthly basis. The man who has not produced a sale for a period of sixty (60) days will be taken off the floor. The man who has not produced an annual income of $10,000 will be asked to resign. To sell real estate you must go through these six steps:

1. Be a CREATIVE THINKER.
2. Get all the facts about the property under consideration.
3. List the property as an EXCLUSIVE.
4. Prepare the facts in sales presentation form.
5. See prospective purchasers and make presentations.
6. Make presentations until you SELL the property.

Let's explain what we mean by the six points listed above.

1. One of the best ways to be a creative salesman is to find a piece of property and figure out how to sell it. In selling homes you must create a desire in the person's mind to want to live in the particular home you have picked out to sell him. You do this by knowing all there is to know about the house, (features, construction, measurements, builder, etc.), neighborhood (including schools, churches, shopping, transportation), and particular section of the city. Much of your time in selling real estate will be spent in creating something to sell an individual. If you don't create your plan well, you will not make very much money as a real estate salesman.

2. Get all the facts about the property under consideration. The entire reason for investing in real estate is the use of someone else's money. It is imperative that you know exactly how to finance a piece of real estate before you ask someone to buy it.

In selling homes, generally speaking, a home that is put up for re-sale will have a definite financing problem. You must know how to do this or it will not be possible for you to sell it.

The facts that a home buyer must have (which means you must have them first) are the location to shopping, churches, schools, transportation; construction, floor plan; type of water, heater, furnace, and carpeting in the house—what kind it is and how long it has been in the house; what is the expected life, etc.

3. List the property as an "Exclusive." To do anything properly you must be in control yourself. Before you can sell a piece of property, you have to be able to deliver it. Most people will not give you their property as an exclusive if you merely ask them to do so. Unless you have a plan, a man who has been smart enough to obtain a piece of property will probably not be so stupid as to tie it up with a real estate salesman unless he is pretty sure that the real estate salesman is going to sell it.

If you make all the necessary plans and attempt to sell a man on giving you an Exclusive, don't waste your time b trying to sell his property unless he does give you an Exclusive.

Obtaining a listing at market price with terms attractive to a purchaser, and listing it as an exclusive, should take 80% of your time. Selling productively and successfully starts with this premise.

Up to this point, your basic knowledge has been simply that of real estate. The rest of the sale is not necessarily confined to real estate as such.

4. Arrange all the facts in logical sequence and prepare them in sales presentation form. The knowledge needed to do this is merchandising knowledge more than just plain real estate knowledge. The presentation you make is what the ultimate customer is going to buy—not the real estate itself. It is absolutely imperative that you get all the information there is about the piece of property under consideration. After you have done this, you are ready to move on to the next step in selling real estate.

5. Seek prospective purchasers and make sales presentations. This is nothing more than just plain selling.

Plain selling calls for seeking out people who might be prospects for what you have to sell, and showing them the particular piece of property you want them to buy, and giving them logical reasons for buying. You are now in a position

where you have to become a professional salesman if you
expect to make money in this business.

6. Keep making sales presentations until you sell the
property. You may be a fine creative salesman, you could have
a property listed as an exclusive, you could have prepared a
beautiful brochure, and you could tell your story beautifully,
but if you can't close the sale, you won't make any money. This
is the area where 95% of the people fail. You must learn how to
close sales presentations.

We feel that as a company we should be able to give you
the "know-how" and leadership to take the six steps outlined
above. Your manager's job is as follows:

1. Tell you what to do.
2. Show you how to do it.
3. Have you do it and correct you where you have not
   understood the "what" and "how."
4. Supervise to see that you are doing the job correctly
   and properly.

The basic premise behind our company is a desire to build
a team that will be "our" company. A team is no stronger than
its weakest man.

We feel that in order to build a stronger company we must
attract the highest caliber manpower. To do this we must build
in our company the qualities it takes to attract and hold good
men.

We feel that one reason most good men leave to go
somewhere else is because they are forced to do it. Their
company fails to give them proper planning or leadership. All
the company does is to take part of the commission when a
man goes out and digs up a sale alone.

We plan to hold up our end as a company by supplying
you with the needed planning, advice, and leadership that it will
take to enable you to make money. IF YOU DO NOT WANT
TO MAKE MONEY, THEN YOU MIGHT AS WELL LEAVE
RIGHT NOW! The only way the company can make money is
by you making money. If you don't make money, the company
won't make money—and this company is going to make money.

Even if we have to put pressure on you constantly to produce sales!

Specialize in one phase of the real estate business and become proficient at it.

Take a look at other successful businessmen and dress as they do.

Attend all self-education seminars or clinics made available by the Real Estate Board, plus other forms of self-education. This is part of your job, not just "we hope you will do it." In all other professions it is necessary to constantly re-sharpen your business tools. The real estate business is no exception.

Drive a good clean car, always. A late model car is not necessary, but cleanliness is absolutely necessary.

Find out what the rules of the office are and follow them by reading the Policy Book.

In a business of this size there are a number of people in the office at different times. If you have business here, fine! If not, do not waste other people's time just because you do not have anything to do yourself. If you pick up the telephone when it is ringing, remember that you are the company.

When a salesman brings a client to the office, the other salesmen should leave the room. The manager's area can be used for that purpose. A client will not talk as freely when he is sitting out in the middle of our office in the presence of other salesmen. Stay out of the room unless you have business to conduct in there.

Your office manager is available to you if you want to talk business. He has, or will find, the time to help you with your problems concerning the selling of real estate. When you do go to see him, discuss your business and then be on your way. He, too, must work.

Special Functions of a Rybka Salesman:

1. List, sell and inspect all listings within your service area within 48 hours. Turn in appraisal to manager on all listings inspected.
2. Ride area assigned every Monday.
3. Call every seller on Wednesday of each week.

4. Call every buyer once a week.
5. Give equal time of effort to outside work, for each floor time.
6. Read realty advertisements daily.
7. Mail out literature immediately. Fill out daily advertising results form.
8. As a listor, or as a selling man, help close all offers immediately.
9. Cover floor promptly and work all assigned days, including Sundays.

_____

Salesman

_____

Broker

Chapter Eighteen

Prepare to Branch Out!

*Today's extensive changes are creating exciting challenges for every practitioner in the real estate field. Probably no one is more aware of this than the broker who finds himself on the threshold of expansion—from one office to several, or from a few offices to many.

Just as every broker continually looks forward to the improvement of his position, his salesmen should be preparing for self improvement. Plan your own career. The time will come when you will want to open your own office and begin branching out to ever greater earning possibilities. In this chapter and the following one, dare to envision yourself as a broker who is studying the advantages of a major expansion.

First, as a determined operator, you would note that the typical homeowner moves every five years; that the average tenant moves at least once annually. At a time when brokers are most interested in the movement of people across the nation, some brokers fail to realize the greatest movement is within a small radius—sometimes merely across town. The great number of people who are moving and the increasing use of computers

---

*The material for this chapter originally appeared in the article "Branch Office Managment," by Edward F. Rybka, in *Real Estate Today* Magazine, July 6, 1969, no. 6. Copyright 1969 by the National Institute of Real Estate Brokers of the National Association of Real Estate Boards, 155 East Superior St., Chicago, Illinois 60611.

in real estate firms give today's real estate man the opportunity to serve people constantly and repeatedly.

Real estate firms of the future will undoubtedly have more sales persons working in each office. There will be larger real estate companies working on a city-, state-, and countrywide basis. More of tomorrow's brokers will be professional business-men in every sense of the word.

Consolidation May Be Cheaper

The real estate business is one of the few remaining endeavors in our present economic system that continues to operate on a small, individual basis. But it can be more economical for one real estate company to have a network of offices, or for several firms to consolidate into one large company, thus eliminating duplication of secretarial work, bookkeeping, attorney's fees, and various other costs. Also, the branch office system offers compensatory advantages, because when one section of town is going through a sales lull, a branch in another section can be in the midst of heavy activity.

Brance offices should be located where the action is. Before a site is chosen, a survey of real estate transfers should be taken. This serves the same purpose as a traffic count for a gas station. If the survey shows that the proposed area has enough sales action, a branch office can be opened.

The size of the branch office building should be large enough to conduct business efficiently and it should also offer space for expansion. Frequently, brokers open offices in build-ings which provide no expansion possibilities and thus the rented space is too small for their potential volume. The office should be on the ground floor, preferably in a corner location, with adequate parking for customers and salesmen. The interior of the office should give the impression of a rather expensive installation—a successful, stable organization. It should be air-conditioned, carpeted, and have acoustical ceilings.

Personnel—Most Important Factor

Having a good physical plant is important. More impor-tant, however, is that the staff be well chosen and well managed. The ingredients for a successful branch office operation are self-motivation, knowledge, field supervision, and a flexible overhead.

The key to the branch's success is the manager. He should be a selling manager so that he can motivate others by power of example. He should be chosen because of his ability to list homes and his record of high production as well as his desire to supervise an office. The manager is the quarterback. Development of the office around him is essential.

The tempo of the branch office is set by the manager. As the key person, he performs all the jobs necessary for a profitable organization. Since other people will follow his lead, he should have thorough knowledge of all the basic functions of the real estate office. He is the person who makes all the listing inspections; he makes his phone canvassing calls daily, drives regularly through his area and keeps his listing folders current. He lists, obtains realistic pricings on properties and makes sales.

The manager should have a trained, licensed staff consisting of at least half the estimated number of persons eventually needed, before a branch office is opened. The number of salesmen in a branch is determined by the population in the area that the office will serve. The real estate business might be considered as a debit business, similar to the insurance business. One real estate salesman is needed for every 2,000 families in the area.

It is not the manager's responsibility to hire and train the salesmen. Sales personnel should be engaged and trained by the main office and then assigned as fully trained associates to the branch. All the manager is expected to do is to transfer his production from one office to his branch and, given the opportunity, to expand that production.

In addition to salesmen and the sales manager, other personnel are needed to operate branch offices. A procurement man serves the branch from the central office. This job is handled by the broker when the office is small but can be delegated when there are numerous offices.

The procurement officer hires and trains salesmen before they are needed and assigned to the floor. He teaches theory and practice with knowledge acquired either from books or his own experience. The instructions include complete information about the service being rendered as well as selling methods. Thus, when a salesman arrives at a branch office, it can be assumed that he is well qualified to handle his particular job.

A multibranch operation requires a general manager who visits each branch office weekly and sees that it is running smoothly and according to sound, fundamental practices. His chief job is to put knowledge into practice. He coaches the staff in using skills effectively, with a minimum of time and effort. His job: teaching know-how.

To free men for sales and listing work, it is important to have an escrow department. The escrow man places all loans with the lenders. After a contract is signed by both buyer and seller, the escrow man's responsibility is to follow the sale through to its legal completion. The listing and selling man no longer has contact with buyer or seller and is free to create new business.

In order to keep the overhead flexible, all of the above-mentioned positions (manager, salesmen, procurement man, general manager, and escrow man) should be paid on a percentage of the gross earnings received by the company or a flat fee per sale—but never a flat salary. This payment plan is important in keeping the company financially sound in fluctuating markets.

Like most branch offices, ours has two salaried employees, a bookkeeper who posts all of the sales journals, writes checks and helps with any office typing, plus a secretary who types the listings and writes all the advertising for the newspapers. The broker should include all office employees in the quarterly review meetings to ensure that a harmonious rapport is being maintained between himself and each member of the firm.

Secrets of Success

Enthusiasm is one of the secrets of a successful branch operation. The capable manager will stimulate his staff to greater action by maintaining a high regard for his staff and their abilities. He should not permit the salesmen to let negative ideas thwart the course of their progress. He should influence them by his own exemplary behavior and PMA—Positive Mental Attitude.

A good manager can freely communicate with his staff. He must be able to observe, probe and search for clues of depression or frustration in his sales staff. He must always be ready to talk to and counsel his members, inspiring them to action through their own self-motivation which, in the final analysis, is the most important ingredient for the continued success of a salesman's career.

The manager also has the responsibility of settling grievances or personality clashes within his staff. Also, if there are any public relations problems with clients, the manager should step in and seek accord and satisfaction of both sides.

Miscellaneous jobs within the branch should be delegated carefully by the manager so that each member of the staff feels that he is a part of the team and needed for more than just selling and listing. The manager should always be willing and able to help his staff whenever they require his assistance or his decisions.

Self-Management

The success of managing a real estate operation rests on the manager's ability to supervise people, yet trust them to schedule their own day. In this way, salesmen are trained to manage themselves. Skillful supervision of sales people is the clue to managerial proficiency. Certain methods work well for our company:

1. A Listing Control Board, showing all the listings of the branch office, is essential. Listings are posted on this board according to expiration date, type of property, and price range. The control board also contains the names of the branch salesmen with spaces for them to "check off" their personal inspections of the properties.

2. Each salesman should have a record stand on his desk which contains manila folders and all of his exclusive listings. In the folder is the advertising and all information needed to keep abreast of each listing. The man-

ager can then see, by glancing at each man's desk, who
has properties for sale, and how many, and who is out
of listings.

3. Each salesman should be assigned a territory of 2,000
families. Within the area, he is expected to make five
listing canvassing telephone calls per day. This assign-
ment helps avoid duplication of efforts and the over-
working of a particular section of town.

4. In a multibranch operation, a teletype service is needed
so that each office can send and receive messages. Such
a service makes the sales staff more conscious of time.
In addition to providing the necessary factual information concerning listings, sales or changes of conditions,
the teletype is used to stimulate new sales and to
confirm that floor assignments are kept.

5. A prized sales stimulator is what we call our "Big
League" board which shows each man's monthly
number of listings and sales over a 12-month period.
Such a board gives a man an opportunity to compare
himself with his teammates. It also affords the manager
an opportunity to see which men are performing well
and where the weaknesses are in the staff.

6. A record of earned income of each salesman should be
kept and distributed monthly to the staff. Real estate
salesmen enjoy competition; they like to see how they
compare with others. Also, such a statement lets the
salesman know just how much he has earned each
month.

7. The monthly sales journal should also be used to chart
profit and loss figures. The sales journal shows the
number of transactions and earnings in each month and
also determines the month's net profit or loss, by
subtracting the expenses for the current month. The
important thing is not the amount of money received in
a particular month, but the number of transactions that
have been completed. It is extremely dangerous to
analyze profit or loss on the basis of checks received,
for they could be from transactions that were in escrow
for two or three months.

With these graphic aids, a manager is able to check individual sales production, to determine who the consistent high earners are or to decide who needs help in improving his earnings and the company's profits.

Aptitude Plus Attitude

The staff's attitude is also the branch manager's responsibility. Proper attitude means success in selling. Real estate men can be trained to do a job, but their performance will be determined by their feelings about their broker, their office and their work. And good aptitude combined with a good attitude makes unbeatable sales people. One of the ways attitude is expressed is in the weekly sales meetings held in the branch office. Here members can exchange ideas and get new ones from inspirational audio-visual aids. These meetings should start at 8:30 in the morning and last only about a half hour. Monthly general staff meetings are necessary too. These sessions give the individual the feeling of being an important part of a large operation which also helps to develop team spirit. The agenda should consist of a company sales progress report and success stories told by individual staff members.

It is important to recognize that highly motivated salesmen need to have the opportunity to manage their office and to earn money in addition to their own listing ability. Denied that opportunity, they may join a competitor. Therefore, each ambitious member of the branch should have the opportunity of becoming the assistant manager without remuneration. This position should not be available until the branch office has been open at least six months.

Extremely important in branch office management is a quarterly review with each member of the organization—a "How Am I Doing?" session. The broker confers privately with each individual in the branch, reviewing listings, listings sold, sales, listing folders and the number of telephone calls made in his territory. The broker should be quick to compliment commendable efforts and to listen to the man's ambitions, problems or any other difficulties. As he listens, he soon will know the trend in office attitudes. Following the individual talks, the broker should call a group meeting and offer whatever suggestions or encouragement that will benefit the staff as a whole.

To brokers, expansion means many things. Internally, because operating costs, wages and advertising expenses are steadily rising, the smallest of companies is forced to grow to maintain a constant profit. Externally, it means keeping a share of the ever-growing market. It is an expanding world and in order to remain competitive, brokers should expand accordingly.

The branch office system offers many advantages over a centralized type of organization. First, it is more efficient because it takes advantage of flexible overhead by having a minimum of straight salaried employees. Second, it affords a competitive advantage in that the salesmen hired are known and live in the area they serve. Third, and most important, it affords a close manager-salesman relationship. Thus, the salesmen keep that positive attitude so necessary for success.

Chapter Nineteen

Managing for Growth and Profit

Many books have been written to facilitate selling and open the secret of making money in real estate. This chapter, based on real estate management, is a bonus for the man who seriously is interested in improving himself and in taking a giant step forward.

Real estate management is an extremely interesting and important facet of the real estate business. This is particularly true for the firm that has overcome its initial hurdles and is continuing to grow and to attain a sphere of influence in the business community.

Let me emphasize that it is the obligation of the broker to outline the methods of achieving the best sales performance as, well as to train his salesmen to adhere to the prescribed system. Furthermore, although there are many good practices for a successful brokerage to follow, one fact stands out. That is that every organization needs a strong leader—the top man or broker who spends the majority of his time establishing major policies and in instituting long-range plans.

Subordinates or office managers will implement the leader's plans and policies. Their job is more in the doing than it is in the planning, although admittedly, some policy making does originate in the lower echelons.

The minimal objectives of every real estate organization are to stay in business and to make some money. Beyond that, to attain a respectable or competitive position, a policy book should be established and circulated. This is true for all types of organizations. Policies must be spelled out if the men down the organizational line are to know and abide by them.

It should be self-evident that nothing can be accomplished until a chain of responsibility is developed and organizational men are charged with specific tasks. At the very top is the broker, the central authority who gives direction to all of his associates. At each level in the real estate organization, there must be a decision maker who will supplement but not supplant the leader's direction. These decision makers are the managers at each branch office or in each department.

Today, people resent being ordered around and this is equally true for persons who are up the ladder or near the top of their organization. The wise president or owner of a real estate company knows that he can demand certain actions or compliances, but he recognizes that it is more prudent to try to win the support of his managers and fellow workers.

The difference between compliance and loyalty is important. Orders do not generate much enthusiasm or strong support. Subordinates will pitch in, work hard and try to fulfill a program they like, particularly if they were permitted to help develop it.

Don't misunderstand this subject of delegating work. When you delegate tasks and all goes well, you get rid of doing the detail work yourself, but you do not eliminate your responsibility in seeing that the jobs are done. It is important to recognize this in choosing managers.

There are two types of managerial authority. One is the "authority of position." The other is "authority of knowledge."

As you know, authority is the right to give orders. A manager who knows nothing about his job can give orders and have authority of position, but it takes more than that to run an office. Technical and administrative know-how are required as well.

A manager's authority of position is much stronger when it is supported by authority of knowledge. The position can command compliance, but it is knowledge that commands respect. The man who possesses both has real authority. Don't overlook this when putting men in managerial jobs.

You never can give any man all the authority he will need to pursue every detail of his operation. At best, making decisions on a managerial level creates a risk simply because all managers will not choose the same solution to a given problem. To minimize the risks, the broker should establish all policies and rules that he deems necessary to guide his subordinates.

The branch manager should have no problem in knowing what to do with the various situations which will arise in his office.

Making Policies Is Not Enough

For the real estate broker, formulating policies is not sufficient. Everyone must know those policies. If and when the rules are established, everyone must be made aware of such rules. Yet, this still isn't enough. You must recheck periodically and lead any who are straying back to the approved procedures. Deciding policy at low levels opens the way to costly mistakes.

Since subordinates do not have rules to cover every situation, it is incumbent upon the broker to decide his company's policies. It is important to remember the exception rule or "exception principle" when establishing policy. Set down rules to cover all conceivable situations. Your managers then decide the routine cases by applying the rules.

But the exceptions—the non-routine situations—are not decided by the managers or even the general manager. The exceptions are to go to you, the broker, for the proper disposition.

When a company grows, there is a need for managers. How many men can one man supervise? The answer is known as the "span of control." A manager's responsibility can be specific, allowing him to control from six to 12 persons effectively. There are two factors which will bear upon a manager's supervisory capability. One is the ability of his men. And the second is the matter of how much time he has to spend on his supervisory work or his demonstrations in the field.

As the real estate company grows, one should recognize that many, or at least some, of the original employees in that company are not sincerely interested in developing the real estate brokerage into a larger profession. Therefore, don't permit the company's growth to be stunted by keeping it under the control of disinterested parties. You also will have to recognize that loyalty and seniority, per se, are not the criterion for establishing a large company.

A word of caution, though. Unless you are in financial trouble, you should seldom make wholesale changes. Continually work on changing your organization and its branch operations, but make your revisions gradually.

When a man retires or resigns, you will make changes in the organizational structure. It is difficult for the broker to build a team of managers who understand all of the daily problems. Therefore, when a company's funds or needs are in the balance, it is extremely important to spend money where it will produce the most desirable results. Only the broker can decide where that shall be. He will consult with no one on the staff directly, nor will he give his managers the feeling that they are making decisions as to how the money is to be spent.

When there are managers, it is important to have staff assistance, or people who are named assistants to the manager. They will relieve the manager of burdensome detail—minor things that don't exactly fit into the daily work of the office manager. The assistant will perform many of the smaller functions. He neither makes decisions nor issues instructions, but he does act for the manager in the latter's absence.

There are advantages and disadvantages in having assistant managers. The disadvantage is that they can create trouble. Some assistants love authority, to act as the boss, frequently trying to belittle the office manager and present themselves as superior replacements.

Assistants should be named, however. Their presence lets the manager know that if he does not value his position, there always is someone else waiting to take his place.

Another cardinal requirement is the establishment of company goals. The outstanding goal, of course, is to build a bigger and better real estate company.

It is good for the broker to build an empire, to strive to make his company larger and more efficient. But he also should be cognizant of the fact that it may not be economical to grow too fast. Therefore, check on the zealous, industrious managers so that they don't become overly ambitious and try to expand too quickly.

In large companies there will be rivalry, often intense rivalry, between managers and salesmen. Individuals will jockey for positions, just as they do in politics. Such struggles for advancement in real estate companies go beyond office walls and into the homes of the sales personnel. Then it is in the power of the wives to help or hinder a company's progress. Hopefully, the women will try to be friendly with each other and will try to preserve protocol. A prudent wife will never invite wives of superiors first. Rather, she will let the superiors' wives extend the initial invitations.

Discreet managers and executives will be wary of out-doing the big boss in matters of residence, auto, mink coat, grand piano, golf club membership, or exclusive school for their children.

Cliques Will Form

The broker also will be cognizant of the fact that in each organization there will be cliques—little groups that exist on all levels, from fledgling salesmen to the veteran coterie of aides surrounding the top man.

Any time the views of one of these cliques are at odds with the objectives of the company, there is the dangerous threat that the latter will be bypassed. Cliques have their own rules; their own code of behavior.

The broker can't do much about an informal organization within his company, but he should not ignore it, either, in making his decisions. Members of such a group may easily be upset by the actions of the broker and decline to do what the company wants or expects.

A company should not make sudden, unannounced changes, nor should it let the grapevine be the messenger subtly spreading the word about things to come. A change in work hours or in office assignments, for example, can be most

upsetting. The change will be better received if the men are told
in advance and prepared for the innovations.

It is the duty of the broker to establish long-range plans
and goals for his company. His managers merely recommend.
He decides. But to be of value, his decisions must be weighed
according to need. He cannot afford to be overly hasty. He
must always question figures and study alternatives. Road-
blocks and dead wood should be removed before they damage
the morale of the organization.

A broker should remember that underlings ape their
bosses. The good broker will consult frequently with his sales
staff to get suggestions and support for his plans. He also will
establish a budget for each office and each division in his branch
operations.

Managerial Power Develops

To achieve stability, list your present executives and their
current jobs and the positions they probably can attain. Know
how old they are. Make a schedule of executive jobs to be filled
in the next five years, together with the vacancies that can be
anticipated because of retirements or resignations, or because
newly created positions emerged too quickly.

Promotions also lead to chains of events. When a man is
promoted, his former position is vacated. That opens the way
for job flexibility which usually extends to the lowest echelons.
To expand rapidly, promote some of your better bottom-level
workers to assistant managers. Present assistant managers may
then be moved up to managers. To contract rapidly, put them
back into their former jobs.

In laying off men at the bottom, others up the line are
demoted. Of course no one likes demotions, but when customers quit buying, overhead must be cut and sometimes,
employment must be reduced.

So, in considering the number of managers you will need
in the future, always train more than enough managers and do it
ahead of time. Have in readiness a few more men than you are
sure you will need. Keep them ready before you need them.

There always are emergency openings in real estate companies due to death, poor health, resignation and unforeseen

expansion. Stability can not happen overnight. It is the result of long-range planning and training and careful analysis at the high level of command.

Resignations also can produce a chain reaction. Never allow a minor officer of the firm to loom so large that his sudden loss will hurt the company seriously.

Two-way communication is extremely important in the company. Avoid a situation in which you are surrounded by "yes" men. Impress your subordinates and associates with your desire for complete truth.

You should, of course, express your own ideas after you have given the subordinates an opportunity to talk. Let them present their suggestions and problems. Perhaps you can follow their suggestions, but never belittle or ignore anyone's suggestions. Do so and you never will get any more suggestions.

Morale Is a Mental Attitude

Morale is affected by a man's attitude; by his frame of mind. When he feels good, he thinks his company is great and he shows it by doing more work. When he has turned sour about the company, he usually does less work and the quality of his efforts slips.

Sometimes he doesn't develop this attitude by himself. He gets it from his fellow workers. If they like the company, he does, too. If they don't like the company, his loyalty falters as well.

Don't overlook the importance of morale. Poor morale doesn't mean that you'll get no work. If you are ruthless enough, you can get work out of men who hate you. However, even the fear of losing a job loses significance when other jobs are plentiful.

High morale equals high production. That has been accepted for years as axiomatic. At times you will see situations where there is low morale, but high production. The worker may hate the boss, but the boss enforces high production. In a real estate organization, enthusiastic men usually are better producers and they do their work with less supervision. In turn, output is higher and costs are lower.

The morale of the managers takes precedence over the morale of the bottom-level workers. An entire department's work will be good or bad, depending upon the work of the manager. Moreover, morale is contagious. You may get to feel the same way the manager does.

A high level of morale can be achieved when the company tries to be fair and reasonable in wages, promotions, concern for all individuals and in the handling of grievances. But be ready to eliminate anyone who tries to make the other workers feel that they are mistreated, or that the management cannot be trusted.

Rules Keep Objectives in Sight

In all real estate organizations there are men who will not do their work properly; who will violate the rules. So you must have penalties, but make it constructive discipline. The men should accept the rules because they understand them and agree to their fairness.

When rules are violated, you must do something, or the rules will be meaningless and you simply will encourage more violations. Institute a grievance procedure through which a penalty decision can be appealed.

Criticism is a minor type of discipline. No one likes to be criticized and you should make sure it is justified before you do it. If criticism is warranted, it should be done privately if possible and never in front of employees of equal or lower rank. When criticizing a salesman, give him an opportunity to save face.

Yet, if a sales person has been flagrantly insubordinate, he should be reprimanded publicly. Others who are aware of his infractions will then know that you did not permit such behavior to go unnoticed.

Normally, though, you should try to soft pedal criticism and offer suggestions as to how future effort or conduct can be improved. It is a matter of trying to emphasize a positive rather than a negative approach. Brokers should try the "sandwich approach." In this approach, the subordinate is praised first for a good deed, then criticized for something bad and finally, praised again for some other good effort—all in the same interview.

The Purpose of Discipline

Discipline is educational and intended to change behavior. The way to administer discipline is first, criticism and a friendly discussion; second, reprimand. A severe reprimand—a penalty—should be made in private.

Hardship or inconvenience should be decided before one deals a penalty. An employee should be discharged only as the last resort. Remember, discipline of all types is negative.

Consider the effect of the discipline on the man and on the total office before administering it. Once a person has been disciplined, that should be the end of the matter. You can and should talk to the man privately and see that the cause of the discipline is not being repeated.

All employees should be on the same base or pay schedule. Bonuses are not common in the real estate business since it is only logical to pay a man what he was hired to do in the first place.

Furthermore, bonuses can go up and down. They can raise the individual's standard of living, but drop it as well. In the latter event, the bonus program deflates morale.

Many brokers do have incentive plans, though. Some try paid vacations. Before you instigate vacation pay, know that paid vacations have a cost factor of about 3% of your payroll.

Some brokers institute profit sharing bonuses. There are good and bad points to profit sharing. It is supposed to have an incentive value—the employees will work harder to earn more. This is true and yet, if a bonus is not tied to any individual effort, it will be so long in coming it will have low incentive value.

Make a Size Decision

Another important decision for the broker is the determination of how large his company should be. Large real estate companies have distinctive advantages over small ones in developing future executives. They usually get first choice of the most talented people in the community.

Large companies also have the advantage of creating a better image, of attracting the better known names of the community and of opening the doors to opportunities for more conducive business terms.

Small companies find it hard to attract young men. They can't provide formal training or varied experience for the development of ambitious people.

One disadvantage of a big real estate company is that its very size makes good management a must. It is a job to control multiple offices. Even with good managers, big companies have disadvantages. They can't adjust quickly to market conditions in terms of advertising or expenditures. Often, they can't give as good or as intimate service as small companies. The type of service the broker would like to extend to his customers is normally not the same type that his salesman or representative will offer.

Furthermore, the big company always is in the limelight. It must be careful of all its actions, that it does nothing to irritate the public. Frequently, large companies will be sued for a minor transgression. Many times, an attorney is waiting for them to do something wrong.

Checking on Personnel

In any real estate operation, the need for careful personnel handling is paramount. Of course, the subject of personnel relations is in vogue today. Indeed, the subject assumes the proportions of a fad and some now are saying its importance is being overdone.

Nevertheless, it would be smart for a real estate broker to make a morale survey to determine what his workers think about the company and its practices. A morale survey could reveal unsuspected gripes, particularly where morale differs greatly from office to office.

Turnover Is to Be Expected

Turnover is also a fact to be dealt with in every real estate operation, large or small. It is to be expected. Employees will come and employees will go, so the broker must realize that he will have to make replacements.

An employer quickly learns that he has to hire quite a few

people to keep his organization at the same size. For factories or industrial work, a 30% turnover is low and 50% is common. In foundries there will be a 75% turnover. This doesn't mean that nearly everyone quits every year. It does mean that some jobs will have to be filled several times in any given year. In general, most companies have a 30% turnover in 10 years.

A real estate broker can expect 20% of his good producers to leave and to open their own companies. He will have to hire 35 men a year to keep his working staff at 100. A turnover of more than 50% indicates he hired too promiscuously.

Turnover—one man leaves and another is hired to replace him—costs money. When a man leaves, less work is done. Moreover, it costs at least $2000 to train the replacement. You cannot eliminate turnover, but you can reduce it and thereby save the cost of constantly training personnel.

The broker tries to cut turnover by finding out why workers quit and by eliminating the causes, if he can. It is advisable, therefore, to have termination interviews with men who are leaving so that you can truly understand the background for their decisions to move.

Promote from Within

Most companies follow a policy of filling vacancies from within, if possible. The promotions from within build morale and are healthy, if not carried to extremes.

There always is a danger that the future of the company will lack its original breadth of background in which case the efficiency of the operation may suffer. People who grow up in a company are likely to have fewer ideas for improvement and they resist change more than those who have been outside the industry and were only recently brought into the organization.

Demotions Seldom Solve Problems

Demotions rarely are effective except where work forces are reduced. The demotion seldom solves the problem when a man fails on the job to which he has been promoted. He does not realize that he is failing, nor does he realize that he is not doing the job well. He does not want to be demoted.

Never offer the choice of being demoted or discharged. This does not work out well. He probably will take the demotion and remain a distraught employee for life. His morale and those around him will suffer. So it is best to avoid the problem by discharging the man rather than demoting him. But if the latter course is to be pursued, then demote him into another office away from his old job and former associates.

What Women Mean to the Company

In building a real estate company with women, be aware that absenteeism will be at least a third higher than it is with men. Turnover also will be much greater. Bell Telephone Co., for example, has 60% turnover among its women employees and less than 10% among the males.

When hiring female employees recognize that the possibility of long production will not be great. Women are more likely to take things personally—to think favoritism is at play. Consequently, better-trained managers are needed to supervise women. The skillful manager will guard against friction and keep things running smoothly, well aware of the fact that women frequently outproduce men.

But with either men or women employees, all workers value proper introductions to the staff. Indeed, without proper introduction to the firm, many employees can't adjust and soon quit. You can reduce this kind of turnover by introducing the new salesman to his manager and to the staff at a formal meeting.

Training on the Job

Nearly all real estate training is done on the job. One exception is in the case of rapid company expansion when special classes have to be organized to speed training. Another exception is a class retraining for jobs. Whenever you wish to retrain personnel, the classes should be called conferences.

Many new and most older salesmen won't admit they need any training, so arrange a conference series instead of a training program and use discussion leaders rather than teachers. These improvement sessions will be better accepted.

Training should be done during working hours. Brain sessions—brain-storming—are important, so break up the sales organization into small groups. Many people are reluctant to say anything at a big meeting, but will open up when they are in a small group. And you must have total participation if you are to have an ideal brain-storming session. Let each member of the group advance an idea.

Vacations Are Important, Too

Vacations are important for the morale of the organization. They benefit the employee and company alike.

Establish vacation periods in advance. Arrange schedules and give workers with the most seniority the priority in choosing vacation dates.

Importance of the Manager

The manager of the real estate company is the most important man in the organization. He represents top management. He should approve the hiring of the individual worker. He should have the power to suggest the firing of employees. He determines and should be consulted when disciplinary action is needed. He has the power to make decisions with the help of top management.

The manager must get the workers off to a good start. He develops the man's sense of belonging to the organization. Actually, the manager has to do the training on the job and he has to develop the work habits. If there are work grievances, they generally concern something the manager has or has not done.

For each salesman, the manager is the main channel of communication. He confers with the salesman on all questions and problems and instructs him in the company's methods and policy. Information the manager passes up the line may enhance his own position.

Managers Also Have Grievances

Managers frequently have the feeling that their jobs are not important. Many complaints of the managers are as follow:

1. You don't give us real authority.
2. You don't pay us enough in managerial bonuses. (The manager should be a working manager, receiving a percentage of net office profits.)
3. You don't show any personal interest in us.
4. We don't get much chance for promotions.
5. You don't tell us what is going on or what is coming up next.
6. You don't ask us our ideas on anything.

There are two types of managers—the production center manager and the employee center manager. I believe that all managers fall into these two classes. I feel that the employee center manager gets the best results. He gets more production from his men with less supervision. Workers respond better to the manager who seems interested in them and not just in the production of his office.

The manager's main job is to get production at reasonable cost. His responsibility is in dealing with men. He must maintain a work force, win the cooperation of the salesmen, encourage suggestions and try to keep morale up and turnover down.

Authority and prestige also are vital. They include, of course, a sign on the manager's office door. Pay him a decent managerial bonus—25% of net profits. Give him a separate office, not just a desk.

The manager should never receive a report of a company decision by the grapevine. If his own decision must be reversed, he should be told so in private. He should announce changes in his office; they should not be announced by someone coming in from headquarters. No one should be allowed to take the spotlight off the manager.

Few men make good managers without considerable training.

Index